Divine Thump

Angels among us during thirty years
with the Beverly Hills Fire Department

A True Story

By Lyle Slater

© 2014 Lyle Slater
All Rights Reserved.

No part of this publication may be reproduced, stored in a retrieval system, or transmitted, in any form or by any means, electronic, mechanical, photocopying, recording, or otherwise, without the written permission of the author.

First published by Dog Ear Publishing
4010 W. 86th Street, Ste H
Indianapolis, IN 46268
www.dogearpublishing.net

dog ear
PUBLISHING

ISBN: 978-1-4575-2820-0

This book is printed on acid-free paper.

Printed in the United States of America

*For My Children
and
Grandchildren*

With LOVE

DEDICATION

I dedicate this book to two very special groups of firefighters.

The first group is the New York firefighters who bravely climbed those twin towers on September 11, 2001, to do their job knowing they were in peril going in.

The second group is the Russian firefighters who responded to the Chernobyl nuclear disaster on April 26, 1986. They knew going in they would pay a heavy price down the road from radiation exposure, but the job had to be done to save the lives of many of their countrymen.

These brave firefighters are my brothers and my heroes, every last one of them.

Lyle Slater
Firefighter/Tillerman, retired
Beverly Hills Fire Department
Beverly Hills, California

A portion of the Beverly Hills Fire Department personnel (Lyle Slater upper left) assembled at Old Headquarters.

ACKNOWLEDGEMENTS

I wish to thank all the people who helped me make this book a reality.

Shirley, my wife of 53 years as of 2014, continuously supported and advised me along the way.

Bill Feller and Jack McGing introduced me to the fire service in 1962.

Madeline Dusky, my life-long friend and former classmate, listened to me tell my stories and encouraged me to write the stories down for my children and grandchildren.

Woody and Amy Fairchild supported me by providing both encouragement and technical equipment enabling me to transform my handwritten words into present form.

Paul Elwyn evolved my storytelling style into a manuscript suitable for submission. He also assisted with photo preparation and publishing information. His wife, Maureen, gave us the title, "Divine Thump."

Retired Chief Bill Daley, a longtime friend, provided me with important information about the City of Beverly Hills and the fire department.

Chief Ralph Mundell gave me carte blanche for the use of BHFD photos to enhance the stories.

ACKNOWLEDGEMENTS

Captain Tim Hayes sorted through and provided me with an assortment of photos and information.

I also want to acknowledge all of my BHFD brothers for their dedicated service. Many of them are mentioned in this book.

My daughter, Sierra Suzanne, and son, Marc, encouraged me along the way and provided feedback about the manuscript.

Most importantly, I acknowledge the Angels among us who protect and guide us every day.

Gary Giacomo, Editor of the C.S.F.A. magazine, who gave me permission to use the cover photo taken by Brian Haymer, September, 1996.

TABLE OF CONTENTS

God Had a Plan 1
Angels at the Creek 2
Born to be a Fireman..7
What it Takes to become a Firefighter 12
First Call 16
First Death 18
The Watts Riot, 1965 20
Black Cloud White Cloud 21
Detroit Diesel 23
Jack Daniels 26
Bob Ward's Unorthodox Exit 28
Boat Fire on the Colorado River 30
Car Fire at Third and Sherbourne 33
The Chandelier..35
Tricks on Ellingsen 37
Full Circle 39
First Bomb Scare 42
Gas Attack at the Beverly Wilshire 44
Third and Palm Fire 46
First Brushfire 49
Angles on the Roof...54
First Broken Leg..56
The Potato Toss...59
The Most Comical Rescue Call 62
Peas and Corn 64
Cat in a Tree..66
Gas Spill at the Beverly Wilshire......................................68
Back from Death, Thanks to Moses 70

TABLE OF CONTENTS

Tea for the Tillerman 73
Angels in the Night 77
One in a 1 Million Chance 79
Three A.M. Office Call 85
Gene Kelly Fire 89
Beverly Hills Drug Bust 92
The Battle of Beverly Hills 95
High-Rise Fire Emergency 97
The Edmund Fitzgerald, November 10, 1975 101
The Boot 106
Lucille Ball 108
LA Gay Fire 109
The Yellow Cab Driver 112
Strange and Sad Things 114
Protecting the President 119
Man from Auschwitz 121
Large Garage Fire and Explosion 123
Fireman or Firefighter 125
Gas Spill in a High-Rise Office Building 128
Waterous Pumps 130
Fourteen-Year-Old Girl Overdose 133
The Slater Sling 135
Arsonist 137
Stabbing at the Beverly Hills Hotel 139
Rocket Man 141
Angels in the Smoke 144
The Best Little City Fire Department in the World, 1989 ... 150
Most Stressful Types of Emergency Calls 152
Out at Home Plate 154

TABLE OF CONTENTS

Ed McMahon 157
Full Arrest on Wilshire Boulevard 159
Straight into Hell 161
Don Rickels Fire in the Fireplace 164
Rodney King Riot, 1992 166
Beverly Hills Movie Details 169
The Strangest Request 171
Danny DeVito 173
Beverly Wilshire Hotel Fire 176
The Fourth of July 178
Four-Year-Old Child Drowning 180
$500 182
Henry Winkler 184
Water Torture 185
Air Bags 187
Power Lines Down on Third Street 189
Beverly Hills Drug Brat 190
Fireman's Grand Prix 191
Transformer Explosion 196
Jack Lemmon 198
The Bird Man of Beverly Hills 199
Car Fire on Wilshire Boulevard 202
It Never Rains in California 204
Slater's Ariel Act 206
Two Million to One Chance 209
Christmas Time at the Waldorf 218
Nine Eleven 220
Blessings in Disguise 225
A Great Run 232

PREFACE

Throughout this book I mention working at the old station or the new station. Beverly Hills has three stations, and I belonged to a small group of guys who were privileged to work in all three old stations, all of the temporary stations, and then all of the new stations.

Old Station 3

This station was converted from a house into a four-man, one-engine company station. It was my first station during my rookie year, 1964-1965. It was small and cozy for four men. It featured dormitory type sleeping quarters and no room for expansion. One perk it did have was a mom & pop grocery store next to it which was convenient for an afternoon cold drink or an ice cream bar. It was located on Robertson Blvd. across from Gregory Way.

Old Station 3

New Station 3

New Station 3 was built on the corner of Doheny and Charleville and was dedicated in 1972. This was a beautiful station capable of housing two engine companies. As of 2014 they have one engine company and one rescue quartered there. It has semi-private sleeping quarters and an inside handball court and covered parking.

New Station 3

Old Station 2

Located at 1100 Coldwater Canyon Blvd., Old Station 2 was a house converted into a two-engine company, eight-man station. It featured dormitory style sleeping quarters. The front room had a large wood-burning fireplace. The city parks department supplied wood in the cold months. We enjoyed roaring fires and played snooker on the snooker table in this room during our down time.

Old Station 2

New Station 2

New Station 2 was located at the same place as the old station, so we were housed in temporary quarters nearby until construction was completed and the station dedicated in 1983. This was a very nice station that could house two engine companies. As of 2014 they have one engine company and one rescue quartered there. The station featured semi-private sleeping quarters.

New Station 2

Old Headquarters

Located at 445 N. Rexford Dr., Old Headquarters Station was a nice, old station, but it had seen its day. It had a drill tower and a drill yard next to it where we did our training. I did rookie training here along with six other rookies in 1964-1965.

Old Headquarters

New Headquarters

The new headquarters facility was built at the same location as Old Headquarters. We were housed in temporary quarters across the street until the new station was dedicated in 1987. The new station was beautiful, featuring everything a fire station should have. Visiting fire personnel referred to this facility as the "Taj Mahal." It had semi-private sleeping quarters and was designed to accommodate women firefighters. The old but beautiful City Hall can be seen in the background in this photo.

New Headquarters

Author's Biography

Following two seasons as a crew member aboard a ship sailing the Great Lakes and six years in surveying, Lyle Slater was drawn to a career of firefighting after spending an afternoon with a Cleveland fireman. From that inspiring afternoon, Lyle would eventually spend 30 years on the Beverly Hills Fire Department in California. He began to feel that the ongoing narrow escapes from death could not be attributed simply to training or to luck. During a severe rain storm at his home in Malibu he felt compelled by some force to rush to a creek where he found a woman and two children trapped in a stalled car about to be swept away by fast-rising flood water. Lyle, his son, and a neighbor saved the woman and her two children. He began to feel that angels were protecting him and his fellow firefighters so that they could protect others. His priest with whom he confided these feelings told him he had received a Divine Thump.

Lyle played a part in significant improvements in practices and equipment in his 30 years as a firefighter. He created the Slater Sling which continues to be used today to assist responders carrying air tanks while climbing high-rise stairways. He also assisted with the creation of the first diesel-powered fire engine that improved response time to fires in hilly terrain, and following a badly orchestrated response to brushfire threatening Malibu, he offered recommendations to assist in the creation of a more effective brushfire strike team organization for the Malibu area. As an Emergency Medical Technician, he along with his colleagues saved many people through CPR. Lyle painted Roman numerals on his helmet, one for each of the 15 lives he helped save.

Lyle enjoyed life to the fullest with his wife in Malibu where they reared their two children. He also enjoyed a 25-year hobby of auto racing. In many ways he experienced the ideal life, living what he considered to be God's plan for him. He enjoyed every day of his 30-year career. The hazardous duty of firefighting, however, contributed to health issues for Lyle. A heart condition caused by prolonged toxic smoke inhalation forced him to retire in 1994 from the job he loved with the Beverly Hills Fire Department.

Years later Lyle used his time during treatments for Myelodesplastic Syndromes to write about many of the events and people in his life and to honor firefighters.

Fireman's prayer

By A. W. "Smokey" Linn

When I am called to duty, God
Whenever flames may rage,
Give me the strength to save some life
Whatever be its age.

Help me to embrace a little child
Before it's too late,
Or some older person
From the horror of that fate.

Enable me to be alert
And hear the weakest shout,
And quickly and efficiently
To put the fire out.

I want to fill my calling
And give the best in me,
To guard my neighbor
And protect his property.

And if according to Your will
I have to lose my life,
Please bless with Your protecting hand
My children and my wife.

God Had a Plan

As I look back over my life I believe God had a plan for me. I did not realize how He was working in my life until one day late in my career I experienced an incident at a creek when I saved a young woman and her two very small children from drowning. That rescue and how it unfolded caused me to feel that there was something working in my life. After that rescue I began to think of my life and career, and I began to see that I was put into the position at the right time to save people, either on a team of firemen or by myself. On the flip side of that I was in the right position to have my life saved and in some cases the lives of fellow firemen in performing our jobs.

I recently held a mini-class reunion in Kentucky and was telling some of the stories to a very dear classmate, Madeline Dusky. She convinced me to write my life experiences down for my kids, Marc and Sierra Suzanne, and also for my two grandchildren, Alexander and Lila.

This is a true story of my journey to becoming a fireman for the city of Beverly Hills and performing the job, which I loved, for 30 years.

Angels at the Creek

It had been raining for about two weeks straight in Southern California during El Niño. I was standing in my living room with my 14-year-old son, Marc, looking out the window as we were having a tremendous downpour. I had never seen it rain that hard in my 30 years in California. The water running off my roof looked like we were looking through Niagara Falls. After about 20 minutes the rain let up and we could see the intersection of Bush and Meritt Drive which made up the north and east side of our 1 1/2-acre lot in Malibu. Our lot was about one mile uphill from the ocean. We could see boulders almost the size of soccer balls rolling down the center of the roadway coming from the fire trail 1/2 mile northeast of us and being pushed or carried by about four inches of water. This water ran past our place into Bonzall Creek about 1/2 mile down hill which then emptied into the ocean about one mile away.

My son said, "I wonder how much water is in Bonzall Creek?" In his 14 years he had never seen any water in the creek.

When the rain stopped I said, "Let's go down and take a look."

My wife overheard us and said, "Give me five minutes to check our outside animals, and then I will go with you."

She went outside, and when she closed the door, it was like a switch went off in my head. I looked out the window again, and I had this greatest urge to go, immediately!

I said, "Marc, let's go."

"What about mom?"

"Marc, we have to go, now." I had never felt an urge like that. It was almost like someone was pushing me out the door.

We got in my wife's car and drove down to the creek. As we approached the first street to our left, Rainsford, the road went down into the creek bed and up the other side to the next street. The part of the roadway going into the creek was concrete and built to withstand this type of weather.

I parked the car uphill from the creek, and we could see a BMW on the road in the creek in about one foot of water. The backup lights were going on and off. I said, "Marc, it looks like that car is stuck in the water."

We ran down to the creek, and I waded out to the car and looked inside to see a young woman inside with an infant in a car seat in front and about a four-year-old boy in the back seat.

She said, "The car won't go backwards or forwards."

I told my son to come into the water to try to push the car backwards.

We tried to push the car out, but it would not budge. Someone from the other creek bank yelled, "Do you need a rope?"

I looked up and standing on the other bank was Nick Nolte, the actor, and another man. I later found out the other man was film producer Frank Capra, Jr. I yelled, "The water is rising so fast we don't have time to do anything except get the three people out of the car, because this is going to be all over in a few minutes."

I told my son, "We have to get everyone out of the car, now." The young boy in the back seat was the easiest to get out, first, so we opened the door, and I picked him up. My son helped steady me, because when I stepped out behind the car the current was picking up making it difficult trying to walk the 20 feet to dry land. When I finally made it out of the water, I ran up to my wife's car and put the boy in the back seat, fastened the seatbelt, closed the door, and ran back down to the creek when a neighbor I did not know ran with me and asked, "Do you need help?"

I said, "Yes, we have to get a woman and her infant out of the car before the water takes the car downstream."

We both waded into the current which now was much stronger forcing us to hold on to each other to get to the car. My son had the door open, and I grabbed the infant and the car seat. The neighbor said, "I think I felt the car move."

I said, "Lady, you have to get out and get out, now!"

The neighbor started to help the woman out. My son helped me with the baby, and as I cleared the back of the car the full force of the water hit me. I thought to myself, *God, don't let me fall with this baby.* I had to shuffle my feet along in very small steps. I could hear boulders rolling around me under the water hoping none would hit me. I finally made it to the water's edge and ran up to the car, put the baby in the front seat, closed the door, turned around, and looked down at the creek. My heart stopped. The car was gone and so were my son, the neighbor, and the woman!

I could not see past the intersection of the street and creek because of trees that lined both sides of the creek. I ran down to the creek not knowing what I would see. I got to the creek, and I saw my son pulling himself up the creek bank. The car was floating backwards half submerged, the headlights visible, about 300 feet downstream. I saw the lady and the neighbor grabbing for limbs, roots, anything to get to the bank. I helped my son up the bank, and then we both ran down stream. We were able to pull them out of the water, and we all made our way back to the road. I got the lady in the car with her two children and told my son that I was taking them home, which was about two miles from there but on the other side of the creek, forcing us to take another route to her house. Hindsight revealed that was the way she should have gone home to avoid the creek. I told my son I would pick him up in a few minutes and asked him to tell the police what had happened. I thanked the neighbor for his help and found out his name, Phil Elwell. I had never met him, even though he lived only about a mile from me.

I took the woman and her two children home. On the way there, we introduced ourselves, and that's when I found out she was Lisa Hilton, related by marriage to the Conrad Hilton family. She was shaking from being wet and cold. She thanked me and said at first she did not realize how much danger they were in. I picked up my son and headed home. On the way my son said, "The police came but they were on the other side of that creek, so Nick Nolte gave the police the information." He told me when the lady stepped out of the car it spun around and knocked everyone in the water.

When I got home, my wife at first was very unhappy with me for leaving her, until I explained what had happened. Then I had to tell her that her car smelled like sewage because we were all wet when we got in the car. I also told her that if I had waited for her to go with us, the woman and her two children would have been washed away downstream because that creek rose from one foot to 7 1/2 feet in less than five minutes. That's how little time we had.

Shortly after I came home a television crew showed up at our front door for an interview. Shirley told them I was shy in front of cameras and would not do an interview.

The next morning the car was found 600 feet downstream up against the creek bank where it had made a 90° turn to the left and sank in about eight feet of water. Rocks, mud and all kinds of debris filled the inside of the car, ruining it.

The Malibu City Council presented commendations for good citizenship to my neighbor, Phil Elwell, my son, Marc, and to me. The Beverly Hills City Council also presented me with a plaque. The Hilton family members we rescued presented each of us with a letter of appreciation and a certificate indicating their honoring of us by planting three groves of trees, one for each of us in our names, in a Northern California forest. They said they wanted to give something that represents life, to honor us for saving their lives.

These recognitions were nice, but emerging more prominently in my mind was the feeling I had coming out of this situation.

Later as I thought about my total experience and the overwhelming urge to go to the creek, I was sure I had been sent by a Divine Power. For the first time I realized that something powerful was working in my life. I talked with a priest years later about that urge to go to the creek, and he said that was a "Divine Thump."

Lyle Slater (right) and his son Marc, stand near the water of Bonsall Creek the day following the rescue after the water had receded.

Born to be a Fireman

When I was growing up I was not the kid who jumped up and down every time he saw a fire engine. I had very little exposure to firemen except on two or three occasions in grade school when the local fire chief from the volunteer fire department would give a fire safety class.

Later in life between the ages of 19 to 25 I worked for two civil and city engineers doing all kinds of surveying. Bill Feller and I were traveling all over the west side of Cleveland doing American Title Association (ATA) work. The work entailed completing surveys for the title company to make sure the property they were insuring was the right house on the right property with no encroachments. We also would take a picture of the property.

We had finished five or six properties when it started to rain, so we sat it out for about a half hour. The rain increased. Bill said, "Let's visit with my brother-in-law. He is a Cleveland fireman, and his station is about a mile down the street from here." So we did. This visit would be a life-changing experience for me. Bill's brother-in-law, Jack McGing, was surprised to see us. He invited us in to the kitchen and poured us a cup of coffee, and after a little while proceeded to give us a complete tour of his station and the fire rigs and equipment.

Because of continuing rain we spent about two hours there, and I must have asked 100 questions about the job. When we left I told Bill, "I know what I am going to do for the rest of my working life."

"You're kidding."

"I'm serious. I am going to do what it takes to become a fireman."

When I was in high school I never applied myself in serious study. I did just enough to get by and graduate. Playing football and dating Shirley, my childhood sweetheart, were my big interests. But my study habits changed when I had to study for something I really wanted.

I attended a school taught by a Cleveland police officer every two years. He would give an eight-week class to potential policemen and firemen. The first day of class the teacher brought in a stack of papers about six inches high and said the stack contained the types of questions that would be asked. I never studied that much before in my life, six to eight hours each day. The study covered math, English, American history, but very little police or fire information, except we had about 100 addresses of city buildings and fire stations located in downtown Cleveland to memorize. Walking the streets of downtown Cleveland locating these addresses and memorizing them I surprised myself. I didn't think I could do that, but I did.

I would study the material after class at night, and Bill Feller would quiz me on that material the next day while I was doing the driving between jobs. We also worked on agility, running, lifting, climbing, pulling, all while being timed. I learned more information in that eight weeks than I had in four years of high school.

The test was given in downtown Cleveland. The night before the test I stayed in a hotel two blocks away. The teacher told us to stay close to the center and not to listen to the radio, to eat lightly, to not drink coffee, and to talk to no one. All of these cautions were intended to keep our brain waves from breaking down.

When I walked into the center on the balcony level overlooking a large hall below, I saw long rows of tables with what seemed to be 5000 men sitting at them. My first thought was, *I don't have a snowball chance in hell.*

This was going to be a long test. I had no idea how many questions were on the test, but the thickness of the questionnaire indicated a bunch. When the instructions were given and the command to start was given, I opened the book and to my surprise the questions seemed pretty familiar. I took all of the allotted time to finish the test and checked over my answers. As I left the building I felt pretty good. I thought I had passed it, but I had to be in the first 500 out of 5000 to get a job within the next two years when the exam results would expire.

Two weeks later I got the results. I was very nervous when I opened the letter. To my surprise I was ranked 31 on the fire test and 41 on the police test. That meant I would be in the first class of about 100, but this class would not be called for about six months, because they had just taken 100 men off the last test before it expired, and they were going through the training class.

Fred Henstridge, a friend of mine I worked with in surveying, moved with his wife, Kathy, to Los Angeles to take a job with the state to be involved in surveying and laying out freeways. They both loved living out there and kept trying to get my wife, Shirley, and me to move out there and join them. My wife liked LA from her days flying there on American Airlines as a stewardess. So we thought we would give it a shot for six months until the Cleveland Fire Department called.

The day we drove away from my parents' house after saying our goodbyes was the coldest winter day in recent history. It was 25 degrees below zero and snowing as we pulled out of my parents' driveway and waved goodbye. As we made our way west the weather improved, and when we reached Arizona the temperature was in the high 70's. People were lying around the pools at the motels. I said to Shirley, "I think we made a good decision." We stayed with Fred and Kathy for a week until we both got jobs and moved in to our own apartment near Fred and Kathy.

Shirley got a job as a secretary for a large company, Utah Construction, which was building an industrial park in the LA area. I spent a couple of weeks visiting fire stations where I thought I would like to work, and I also learned about their test procedures. I was interested in eight cities, including Beverly Hills.

Then, Shirley was able to procure a job for me through her boss who put in a good word for me, and I went to work for a soils engineering firm, the Donald R. Warren Company. They had done soils testing for Utah Construction. I did this for about two years while taking fire department tests. About six months into this period, the Cleveland Fire Department called to ask if I still wanted the job in Cleveland. I told the chief thanks, but I was testing to be a fireman in Southern California. So I let that job go. I was on six lists of potential fireman hires when Beverly Hills called me for a job. That was the happiest day of my life, except for the day I married Shirley and the birth days of my two kids, Sierra Suzanne and Marc.

I think I was born to be a fireman, because I enjoyed going to work every day for 30 years.

I recently talked with Bill Feller. I was surprised that I was able to contact him after some 50 years had passed. He was surprised to hear from me. He had heard that I had become a fireman in California, and he asked how I did on the Cleveland test. I told him I was #31. He said he must've been a good question quizzer, and I told him he was. He told me that his fireman brother-in-law, Jack McGing, had passed away about ten years ago, and I said I was sorry to hear that and told him that he and his brother-in-law changed my whole life for the good. I thanked him for that. We vowed to stay in touch.

Lyle Slater's rookie class, 1964-65, (left to right front row) McElroy, Renfro, McKnight, (top row) Capt. Donahue, Anderson, Slater, Davis, Kozak, and Chief Cass

What It Takes to become a Firefighter

Firefighting is a profession like no other in the world. Candidates must really want this job to jump through all the hoops required. First, candidates take a long, tough entry exam competing with a large number of participants for a small number of positions. I have taken tests where I was competing with 5000 other job seekers for 500 openings available in a two-year period. I also qualified in a process involving 300 people for 10 positions in a two-year period when the list expires and you have to re-test if you are still interested in working for that particular city.

If you pass the written exam you will take a strenuous agility test that consists of running, pulling, climbing, carrying heavy objects, and rigorous calisthenics with everything being timed. If you pass these tests you move on to a complete medical physical to make sure you are fit for this demanding job. If that goes well you will be required to take a psychological test to see if you are the type of person to perform this type of work. Then you are required to go through a very thorough background check. No arrests, no drug or alcohol history or any other problems are tolerated. Then you come before a panel of four to six fire personnel, mainly captains and chiefs, for oral interview. You have to convince them why you want to be a firefighter. That's a lot of fun.

If you make it this far, you receive a number score and your name is put on a list according to the grade you received. You wait for the call, which can take up to two years when that list expires. If you are called in that two-year period and have not been hired by another department and still want the job, you will be interviewed by a chief who you will be working for. If that goes well, you will receive all of your equipment, including helmet, turnout coat, Bunker pants, boots, and your badge. You are told where to buy your uniforms, a date for reporting to duty, and which station to report to.

Then you start your learning curve. For one year they send you to the training tower for six weeks to learn hose lays, ventilating procedures, firefighting tactics, medical procedures as an EMT, and much more. You are a rookie for one year, and they make it tough on you, like boot camp in the Army, to see if you have what it takes to get along with other fire personnel. You are being graded and analyzed all the way.

At the end of that year all the captains and the chiefs get together and decide if you made the grade. Now after all of that who the hell wants this job? While most people would not like this job, nor could they do it, the few who do want the job for the next 30 years will be running into situations that everyone else is running out of, and because of that they have to become a jack of all trades and a master of most.

Firefighters acquire knowledge of electrical building construction, plumbing, different roof layouts, and they must operate over 300 tools and much more. Most of this learning will be through on-the-job training from the experienced guys, because not all answers are in the books and firefighters need a lot of common sense, which is not in the books, either. If asked you are required to become a paramedic and take a test every two years to be re-certified. You will become a proficient fire inspector, because you will be inspecting every building in town many times in 30 years.

If you visit a fire station, you'll be impressed with how clean and shiny and neat everything is. There are no maids around, so if you have not picked up your mother's good cleaning skills you will be taught. If you have not acquired your mother's cooking skills you will be taught by the best cooks on the department and never put out a bad meal. If you think the chefs on the TV programs are tough on the participants, wait until you have 25 hungry firemen on your ass if you screw up. You may never live it down.

For instance, one of the firemen, Willie, who by the way was an excellent cook, one day prepared one of his specialties, liver and onions. When preparing the liver, he did not realize that the guy cleaning the kitchen the shift before accidentally mixed up the tub of flour with the tub of Bobo, a cleaning product like Comet that looked the same. That evening everyone sat down for a delicious meal, but as the guys started to wear off the enamel on their teeth, they realized what had happened. Although it was not his fault, he never lived it down, and I am still writing about it some 30 years later.

I will say one thing about firehouse cooking. Other than my mom's cooking, which was the best, the next best meals I have ever eaten were cooked by firemen, and that's because every rookie fireman coming on brings in four or five family-favorite recipes. He is taught how to perfect them by our best cooks on the department. So if you were to work at a 25-man station, you can see how many excellent and different meals you could enjoy.

If you put in 30 years as a firefighter you can expect to have many injuries, big and small, and if you're lucky you'll retire without a disability. For me it was the greatest job in the world but with many injuries.

Firefighter Lyle Slater's shoulder patch

First Call

I was a rookie the second day on the job in October of 1964 when I was stationed at old Station 3 located on Robertson Boulevard. I say, "old station," because a few years later they tore it down and built a beautiful two-story station at another location on the corner of Doheny and Charleville.

The old station was a single-story house converted into a fire station. Capt. Comer, my first captain, was the oldest and most experienced captain on the department. Duke Ellingsen was the acting engineer, and Sandy Patrizio was the other fireman.

At about 9 p.m. we received a call about smoke in a boiler room in an apartment building in the south end of town. I was very excited to go on my first call. At this time both firemen rode on the rear tail board holding on to a handrail that went across the hose bed about eye level in front of us. This was a little dangerous if you got into an accident, and a few years later we started to get new OSHA-required jump seats behind the captain and engineer for the firemen to sit on, which was much safer.

Sandy Patrizio and I climbed on the tail board. Sandy put on his 15-minute air tank. Back then the department did not have air tanks for everyone. Most of us were outfitted with charcoal re-breathers which required a certain amount of oxygen to work properly. It would be another couple of years before the 30-minute self-contained breathing apparatus would be implemented in our department, which would be the biggest improvement in the fire service.

We responded to an old apartment building and the captain called for me to go in with him to check it out and for Sandy to bring in the hose if we needed it. When the captain and I entered the basement we encountered heavy steam, not smoke. The visibility was zero, and we had to feel our way around while bumping into things. We heard a loud hissing sound, and we headed for that when the captain a few feet in front of me yelled out in pain and told me to stop. He received burns on his hands from a very hot spray of steam under high pressure. He said, "Let's get down on our hands and knees and crawl under the escaping steam and try to find a shut-off valve." Because of his years of experience he was able to find it fairly fast.

When the steam cleared, the pressure gauge was way in the red, and the captain said we were lucky that the tank had not exploded on us. He had been around a long time and seen just about everything, and I was glad to be with him on that first call. When the captain had shut the boiler completely down and deemed the area safe, he informed the manager to get a qualified repairman to properly fix the boiler.

We drove to the aid station to get some treatment for the captain's burned hands, then returned to the station. Later that evening the captain took me aside and told me he was impressed with how I handled myself on my first call. "In the situation we were in not being able to see and not knowing what to expect, you stuck right with me. I think you have what it takes to be a good fireman," he said. Coming from him that was a very good compliment. As I worked with him for over a year, he taught me many important things, and the more I worked at this job the more I realized this was the occupation for me. I would spend the next 30 years going to work and enjoying every day of it. I believe God's plan for me was to be a fireman.

First Death

I had been on the job about three months, assigned to old Station 3, when during lunch we heard a very loud hammering on the front door and someone hollering "Help!" We all jumped up and opened the front door to see a young woman saying a man had been hit by a truck, and she pointed across the street. The engineer grabbed the equipment we might need, and we ran across the street.

A middle-aged man with his five-year-old grandson had parked his car in front of our station. He had left his grandson in the car and crossed the street into a business that takes messages for people. He had picked up his messages and walked out the front door when a woman driving past cut a truck off causing the truck driver to jump the curb and nail this guy on the sidewalk. We found him under the truck bleeding from the mouth and gasping for air. We pulled him out as gently as we could and cleared his airway. He was pretty well broken up and was dying on us. The plan was to transport him as fast as possible to the aid station in Beverly Hills, a short distance away. Engineer Ellingsen informed the Beverly Hills police who were on scene that the man's grandson was in the car across the street, and they handled that situation.

The man died on the way to the aid station, and doctors pronounced him dead on arrival. This was years before the paramedic program would be started, so there was very little we could do for him, because we did not know CPR. Our knowledge was not much more than advanced first aid. We used to call it "scope and run to the aid station." The man killed by the truck was the first person I worked on who died, and I felt bad about this and it bothered me for a while. I talked to Captain Keith Comer who had been on the job for a long time. He told me that I could not let this situation bother me if I were going to be in this profession, because it would eat me up.

He said, "You give the very best treatment within your knowledge base, and it's up to God from there on in." That advice was good. It worked for me throughout my career. The paramedic program begun in 1971 was the best initiative ever installed in the fire service. Later on, all fire personnel had to become certified as Emergency Medical Technicians (EMTs). Because of that training we were able to save many lives over the years. Our paramedics were the fifth department in the nation to be trained, behind LA County Fire, LA City Fire, Inglewood, and Miami, Florida.

The Watts Riot, 1965

I was a rookie stationed at old Station 3 when the Watts riots broke out over a police altercation in the East LA area. The riots quickly escalated toward the Beverly Hills area, and the Beverly Hills Police Department shut down the city's eastern border letting no one in or out, and put Beverly Hills on a curfew.

During this time we locked our stations for the first time and patrolled our districts. The rioters never entered our city, but they torched many businesses in East and West LA. Rioters also torched a large building near our eastern border just inside LA territory. Our department responded to assist LAFD in fighting the fire.

Bill Daley, a good friend of mine and fellow fireman, was hired by Capt. Sanchez of our department to protect a furniture store in East LA. Bill took his large black Labrador, Colonel, and a shotgun and stayed there in the furniture store on guard overnight. He had quite a time when some looters entered the store.

This riot was a big deal in its time but nothing compared to the Rodney King riots which broke out years later. I was also involved in that riot and that is another story.

Black Cloud White Cloud

*F*irst-year rookies with a fire department are continually evaluated and can be let go at any time if they do not perform well. Rookies also get a nickname like "Black Cloud" or "White Cloud." Some guys can work one to two years and never go to a major fire. They are called "white clouds." Then there are some new guys who seem to get in on all major fires, and they are called "black clouds." I was tagged a black cloud.

One night I came to work for Art Davis who was going to Mammoth Mountain to do some snow skiing. I arrived at the station at 6 p.m. to take his place and put my turnouts (my firefighting equipment) on Engine 5, the rig I would be riding that night.

I overheard some guys nearby saying, "Black Cloud is here. We will be working tonight." I was in time for supper which was served about 6 p.m. We enjoyed a good meal of fried chicken and the works, watched some television and retired around midnight.

About 2:30 a.m. lights came on, bells started ringing, and everyone in the dormitory jumped out of bed, into boots and Bunker pants, and slid down the fire pole. The watch office personnel said we had a structure fire on Wilshire Boulevard. We responded down Rexford and made a left-hand turn onto

Wilshire Blvd. and down about a 1/2 mile on the south side of Wilshire. We could see fire billowing out of some business street level, and when we arrived on scene we could see it was a bar that had just closed. It looked to be fully involved with fire from front to rear. Fireman Tom Crewse and I took a 2 1/2-inch hose through the front door fighting fire from the sidewalk on in. Engine 3 took a heavy line in through the back door.

The four inches of water coming out the front door was so hot it was burning our knees through our heavy Bunker pants. When we tried to kneel down, the hot steam about burned our ears off. That was before we had nomex socks to cover our head, ears, face, and neck. We found out later that Engine 3 had the same problem with hot water. We were probably making it tough on each other fighting the fire from the opposite directions. After about ten minutes the fire was out, but there was not much left to burn.

As we started the overhaul process, something wet hit me across my face mask. The smoke was still pretty thick so I took out my flashlight and scanned in the direction it came from toward the bar area. I found a beer tap that was partially burned off and was shooting foam and beer across the room. I opened a cooler nearby and found an ice-cold pitcher and lifted it into the spray and filled it up with foamy beer. I was so hot and thirsty I drank the whole thing down, and to this day that was the best beer I ever drank. I have no idea what brand of beer it was. After our overhaul, we gathered at the curb for a smoke. That was just before I quit smoking, somewhere around 1970. We picked up our equipment and returned to the station and had a cup of coffee. It was about 4:30 a.m. I took a quick shower, retired to bed and slept soundly until someone on the oncoming shift woke me up and said, "Time to go home, Black Cloud." I had a cup of coffee and got more razzing from the guys about being a black cloud. I said we were just doing what we get paid to do.

Detroit Diesel

I was working at old headquarters station, riding Engine 5 when at about 11 a.m. we had a general alarm for a structure fire at the top of Truesdale, the highest hill in Beverley Hills. This hill is so steep that our response speed was about eight mph climbing the hill. Children would run alongside of us carrying on conversation.

Chief Tarquinio and his driver in their Suburban could climb that hill at 50 mph. When they arrived on scene ahead of the equipment they found a house pretty well involved with fire.

The owners of the house were pretty excited and shouted at the chief and his driver to do something. He explained, "I can't do a thing until my equipment gets here." They could hear us coming, but it would take us another five minutes to get there. It must've seemed like an eternity. We finally arrived on scene. Engine 2, Engine 5, Truck 4, and Engine 6 went into action with Chief Tarquinio directing.

About two hours later we had the fire out and site overhauled. After picking up all of our hose lines and equipment we returned to the station where the chief called a meeting in the dining room and explained how embarrassed he was standing there waiting for the equipment to arrive with the owners screaming in his ears.

The chief said that had happened enough times that he was going to do something about it. "I am going to look into putting a Detroit diesel engine into a fire engine to improve the response time on all of our hills," said Chief. Detroit diesels had been in trucks before, but never in a fire engine.

The chief and his head mechanic, Hank Bender, spent the next few shifts working on the diesel project, and they came to the conclusion it could be done. So they called Detroit Diesel and told them what they were going to do and to send them a 6V 71 Detroit diesel engine as soon as possible. About a week later the engine arrived at headquarters station. The chief called everybody together and explained that four men from A shift and four men from B shift would be working under the supervision of Hank Bender and himself.

He said, "We are going to re-power this older American LaFrance fire engine that has a gas engine and install the new diesel engine." So for the next few months the team took out the old gas engine and made all kinds of modifications to install the new diesel engine, which was not an easy project.

The day it was finished happened to be on the A shift, which was mine, and because I was one of the team members I was invited along with the other three guys by Chief Tarquinio and Hank Bender to go up to Truesdale to observe this special event.

Chief Tarquinio along with Engineer Bender drove the rig to the hill, and the rest of us followed in a fire prevention car. They started up that hill in a cloud of black diesel smoke and you could hear that engine roaring up the hill and out of sight. A few minutes later you could hear them coming down the hill with the jake brake slowing them, and as they got into sight I could see by the smiles on their faces that they were impressed. They said they had reached a speed of about 38 mph, which was 30 mph faster than the old gas engine.

The story goes that when Chief Tarquinio got back to the station he called Detroit Diesel and talked to their head engineers and told them what he had done. A few shifts later three or four top people from Detroit Diesel Company arrived, and Chief Tarquinio and Hank Bender took them to the hill and gave them a ride. When they returned they were so impressed one gentleman pulled out a pen and told Chief Tarquinio to write his own ticket. They wanted him to work for them. The story goes Chief thought about it for about ten seconds and said, "Thanks, but no thanks. I like my position as a chief on the Beverly Hills Fire Department, but I will confer with you anytime on how I put it all together."

Chief Tarquinio made a big improvement in the fire service. Today, every new fire rigging sold has a diesel engine installed. There are many advantages to having a diesel engine in a fire rigging. They run cooler, have no spark plugs, are more economical, last longer, and are much more powerful.

Years later after Chief Tarquinio had passed away Roger Penske bought the Detroit Diesel Company and built the California Speedway. Days before the opening ceremonies, Roger Penske contacted our Chief Clarence Martin to see if he could have the old 1928 Ahrens Fox that had just been restored to be in the opening ceremonies parade. Penske wanted to honor Chief Tarquinio for what he had done for his company and for the people of Beverly Hills.

Chief Martin refused explaining that the Ahrens Fox was down for repairs and would not be done in time for the ceremonies. When I heard about this I was extremely disappointed. I thought Chief Tarquinio should have been recognized for his contribution to the fire service and Detroit Diesel. This story hopefully brings some light to that history.

Over the years when I worked for Chief Tarquinio he became a friend, and he was a good chief to work for. He passed away way too soon.

Jack Daniels

It was early in my career, and I was working at old Station 2 in early afternoon when we had a general alarm for a structure fire in our district. Captain Dutton Williamson, Engineer Duke Ellingson, Fireman Bob Davis and I responded to this large mansion. When we arrived smoke was showing. The captain, Bob, and I took a 1 1/2-inch hose through the front door. As we made our way into the structure the smoke was banked down to about 18 inches from the floor. At that point we got down on our hands and knees, and we could see clearly all the way across the next two rooms. The fire seemed to be in that second room. As we were crawling through the first room, over in the corner we could see two sets of fireman's boots from the knees down standing together. As we got closer we recognized Johnny's voice. He was a crusty old guy, and he was giving the rookie, Mike, a lesson standing at the bar on how to down a shot of Jack Daniels with breathing apparatus on. That was funny. I laughed to myself.

The three of us continued crawling toward the next room. We could tell we were getting close to the fire, because our ears were getting hot. This was before we had nomex socks to protect our head and ears. We got to a large doorway of the room where the smoke was almost to floor level, but we could see that the other side of the room was fully involved in fire. I turned on the nozzle with a semi-fog pattern and rotated it in a clockwise fashion. A large ball of steam came at us and singed our ears.

About this time we were joined by another crew with their hose line, and we had the fire out in no time. The fire was pretty well contained to this one large room, but there was substantial smoke damage throughout the house.

After we overhauled the fire and returned to the station we shared the story about Johnny giving a class on Jack Daniels to the rookie. Duke sure got a laugh out of that and kept saying, "I can't believe it."

A couple of shifts later we were at headquarters for a training film, and I ran into Mike and said, "Hey, Mike, you have to show me that Jack Daniels technique sometime."

He smiled kind of sheepishly and said, "How did you see us in all that smoke?"

I said, "I'll tell you about it someday." We never did discuss it.

About a year later Mike left the department to pursue a new career, and Johnny retired a few years later. Johnny was quite a character and the oldest fireman on the job when I came on, so he had a lot of funny stories he would tell about his long career with the Beverly Hills Fire Department back in the day.

Bob Ward's Unorthodox Exit

At old headquarters around 9 p.m. we responded to a structure fire in the north end of town. A grease fire that had gotten out of control was confined to the kitchen and dining room.

Engine 1 attacked as Engine 2 arrived on scene a minute later. Bob Ward, the senior fireman on Engine 2, along with Fred Lenert and I were told to take a 1 1/2-inch hose up into the large attic to check for any extension of the fire.

We were making our way through heavy smoke. Bob had the nozzle and I was behind him with Fred behind me. We were looking for fire when I heard a crash like glass breaking. I took another step or two and realized Bob had crashed through a low window which I almost fell out, myself. Bob fell about 12 feet to the ground.

Fred and I looked down with flashlights and saw Bob slowly getting up. I yelled asking if he were okay. He said, "I think so, but I feel like I have been hit by an 18 wheeler." Fred and I could not believe what had happened. Bob later said he tripped on something to cause him to fall forward and then crashed through the window. When he hit the ground the fall broke off the valve on his air tank and it sounded like a jet, and he thought hc was going to take off. He would be sore for a week.

He was very lucky. He definitely had somebody looking out for him that night. I have seen people fall half that distance and be seriously hurt. The fire never got into the attic, and other than a lot of smoke damage the fire never extended past the two rooms.

When Bob retired about ten years later the tradition at our fire department was for the retiree to pick a person to cook his last supper and all shifts and off-duty personnel and retirees would be invited. It was quite a deal. After supper the retiree would be roasted by anyone who had a funny or embarrassing story to tell about the retiree.

The emcee that night was Capt. Stan Speth who told this story about a young rookie (me) who was so disturbed about Bob Ward falling out of a second-story window that he invented a special parachute that Bob was to wear any time he entered a tall building above the first floor.

So I presented the parachute to Bob in front of everyone and we had him try it on. It was like a small backpack with two shoulder straps, a white sheet rolled up on his back with a ripcord on his chest. After he put it on Stan explained that if he ever were to fall out another window, he just had to pull the ripcord. We had him try it to make sure he understood how it worked. He pulled the ripcord, and the sheet unrolled all the way to the floor. Bob looked so funny standing there that everyone was roaring with laughter.

I can't believe how much off-duty time I spent making that thing for one minute of laughter, but it was worth it. I am not sure if he ever took it home to show his wife, along with other things he received, or whether he simply threw it away. It was a fun night. Everyone on the department kicked in money to buy something really nice for the retiree, such as golf clubs, a toolbox, or just cash.

I would see Bob from time to time at the fire department picnics, retirement dinners or Christmas parties. I enjoyed working with him. He was a good friend and a good fireman, and I will never forget his unorthodox exit.

Boat Fire on the Colorado River

I had a 17 1/2-foot Schieta flat-bottom ski boat with a 427 Chevy Corvette engine that could push the boat to a top speed of just over 100 mph. My wife and I made many three-day trips to the Colorado River about 300 miles from LA with mostly fellow firemen and their wives. Most of them learned how to ski behind our boat. I also made one or two trips a year with anywhere from 4 to 12 firemen. This story is about one of those trips.

I brought the boat to the station and after our work day was done the four of us going on the trip prepared the boat. The next morning at 7:30 when our reliefs came in, Craig Tatro, Terry Chavis, Bill Lucas, and I headed for the Colorado River for four days. We stayed at a nice place right on the water called the Thunderbird Lodge.

On the first morning we all enjoyed a good ski ride, and around noon we were sitting on the dock enjoying a cold beer. About 500 feet up river a couple of guys gassed up their boat and headed back to their campsite when about halfway across the river their boat caught fire. We could see both guys bail out over the side with no preservers. All four of us piled into my boat and headed toward them.

When we got close I told Craig to take over my boat. Bill Lucas and Terry Chavis threw the guys some preservers, and

I grabbed a bleach bottle with the bottom cut out which makes a good scooper for bailing water out of my boat in case I take a big wave over the side. In this case it was going to be used as a fire extinguisher. I climbed onto the bow of my boat and told Craig to put me on the bow of their boat and then pick up the two guys in the water.

I started throwing water on the fire. With each scoop I was throwing about half a gallon of water, and it made about an 18 inch spray. Their boat was open in the back, and I could see the gas tanks and hoses were burning. I kept throwing water on it, and after about three or four minutes I had the fire out. Greg picked up everyone, and everybody was okay. We towed their boat to their campsite.

As we got ready to leave, the owner of the boat after many thanks asked us if we were going to Foxy's that evening. Foxy's was a favorite watering hole on the river. I said, "Sure, everyone goes to Foxy's."

He said, "We'll meet you there around 6 p.m. We owe you some beer."

I said, "Very good!"

So after a good supper of baked potatoes, steak, and corn, along with a good salad which we prepared at our dock, we headed for Foxy's. When we arrived the two guys were there, and we could not buy a beer all night. They were grateful for what we had done. We told them we were firemen 24 7. That's what we do. While we were all enjoying beers together the owner of Foxy's, Jerry, who I knew very well, said there were three LA firemen across the dock, that we might want to say hello to them.

After Terry and I finished a few beers, we went over to introduce ourselves to the LA firemen. I said, "I understand you guys are LA firemen." They said they were. I told them Terry and I were Beverly Hills firemen.

One guy said, "That's your tough shit."

That caught Terry and me by surprise. I thought that needed a response, so I hollered back to Jerry, the bar owner, and said. "I thought you said these guys were firemen."

He said, "They are."

I told him, "They can't be, because they are behaving like a bunch of impolite a-holes." Terry and I had enough beers that we were ready for anything. The LA firemen didn't respond. We walked back to the bar and explained what happened.

In all the years I was a fireman and talking to other firemen from different departments, I never experienced any disrespect like what we heard at Foxy's. Later on one of the guys came over to apologize. We accepted the apology. I told the guy, "That loudmouth you have with you is not a very good PR man for your department."

All in all we had a great water skiing trip, and we returned to work with some stories to tell.

Car Fire at Third and Sherbourne

We lived near the corner of Third and Sherbourne just outside Beverly Hills in the Los Angeles area. My wife, Shirley, and I managed a new 24-unit apartment building that we lived in and was built and owned by Chief Cass and Capt. Sanchez, two guys on the department. I was hosing down the subterranean parking area one morning when a Japanese gardener who was working across the street at the intersection of Third and Sherbourne came running down into the garage area very excited. In his broken English he told me a car in the intersection was on fire. He had some hose while doing his work, but it wasn't long enough to reach the fire, so I grabbed a 100-foot hose and we ran to the burning car.

When we got to the street about 100 feet from the intersection I saw the car fully engulfed in flames and a large crowd gathered on sidewalks at the intersection. The gardener and I hooked up the two hoses so we had plenty of hose to go all around the car. I attacked the fire in the engine compartment by putting the nozzle on full fog and shoving the hose under the engine compartment. We could not get near enough to try to open the hood. About this time the front tire on the other side blew out sending the Japanese gardener running to the screams of the crowd. He did return shortly, and I could hear LA Fire coming in the distance.

By now the fire was in the passenger area and going to the trunk where the gas tank was located. Some of the windows were broken out, so I had good access to the interior and was able to snuff the fire out about the time the LA rig pulled up. The car at this time was just a big smoldering pile of junk.

The LA fire crew thanked us. They kept looking at the small garden hose and then at the car. I could tell by their expressions they could not believe that two concerned citizens could have put that fire out with a garden hose. To tell the truth I was surprised we could do it. I rolled up my hose, thanked the gardener for getting involved and left. I was not going to give them the satisfaction of knowing I was an off-duty fireman. I left them thinking two concerned citizens did a pretty good job on that fire. As I walked away I had a smile on my face thinking back to the incident at Foxy's on the river involving three LA firefighters a few months earlier.

The Chandelier

I was at old Station 2 when at around noon we responded to a structure fire in our northern district. We were first on scene by quite a bit and saw heavy smoke coming out the open front door of a large single-story home. Captain Ron Savolskis called for 1 1/2-inch hose line, so I grabbed the nozzle and a couple loops of hose and headed for the front door. Steve Hoffman, the other fireman, grabbed a couple of loops and followed me. As we were advancing the hose a police officer trying to help picked up a section of hose as I was stepping over it, and I tripped falling on my right knee on a brick sidewalk just ten feet from the front door. It felt like my kneecap was broken. I picked myself up and Steve and I, favoring my knee, entered the front door. The smoke banked down to about two feet from the floor, so we crawled down this hallway under the smoke to where we could see fire coming out of what turned out to be the master bedroom. We hit the fire at the doorway and slowly worked our way in. After a few minutes everything pretty much went black with smoke.

Steve and I hesitated for a minute to catch our breath, and we heard a large crash of glass which bounced off the floor. Debris hit our helmets and face masks. We thought maybe it was a skylight, but when the smoke cleared a little bit we realized it was a large crystal chandelier that probably weighed 100 pounds or more. It had come loose from the high ceiling in the bedroom and crashed to the floor about eight feet in front of us. It's a good thing we had hesitated before crawling any farther or we would have been wearing that chandelier.

Steve said, "Who the hell has a chandelier that big in a bedroom?"

I said, "Somebody with more money than they know what to do with."

You never know what you're going to encounter in a fire situation, especially when you have zero visibility. It definitely is an adrenaline rush. Was that good luck or something else?

Before we left the scene my knee was hurting so badly I could hardly walk. Rescue was called, and they took me to the aid station. My kneecap was not broken, but it swelled up just below the knee creating what was called "water on the knee," and it had to be drained. I was off work for a couple of shifts and thankful that the chandelier had not made my situation much worse.

Tricks on Ellingsen

It was around 9 p.m. at old Station 3 when I was working with Capt. Comer, Engineer Duke Ellingsen, and Craig Tatro. I had been on the department about 18 months. We were all watching the Dodgers game. Duke was a big Dodgers fan. His son was a pitcher on the Dodgers farm team and was about to move up to the big time. Duke knew Tommy Lasorda, and he would tell us some interesting stories from time to time.

The best way to get Ellingsen's goat would be to turn the TV off while he was intensely watching the game. On this particular night the Dodgers were not doing very well, and we had not been on any fire or rescue calls. This was unusual, because Engine 3 was for the most part the busiest engine. Craig and I were bored out of our minds. So we thought we'd play some tricks on Ellingsen, who always was a good sport and fun to work with.

Craig was dating this beautiful stewardess who flew for American Airlines all over the world. So we got an idea to compose a letter and make it sound like it was a female admirer of Duke. The letter would have inside information about some funny things that Duke had done in the past. We spent the next couple of hours brainstorming about these funny things and putting them into a letter form.

The next day Craig took the letter to his girlfriend and had her mail it back to Duke from a foreign country, wherever she would be flying next. In a few days there was a letter mailed from London to the station for Duke. He opened it and was puzzled. He got the biggest kick out of it, but he could not figure out what was happening and wondered how anyone could know this information.

Craig and I sent four or five of these letters. Every time Duke would get one he would tell us he had another letter and the country from which it was mailed. He would read it to us and Craig, the captain and I would act as surprised as he was. One day we were all working up at Station 2, and Duke received a letter with quite a bit of postage due. Duke was a little tight, so he refused to pay.

Craig and I fired off another letter that night. The next morning his girlfriend flew to France, and in a few days he received our letter and opened it. Inside was a note with a couple of bucks in it. The note read, "Here's a couple of bucks, you cheap screw, for the next time you are short on postage!" We all started laughing, including Duke, and he knew we were the culprits. He shook his head. He couldn't believe we would spend that much time playing a joke on him.

Duke was a lot of fun to work with, and we stayed together as a crew for about a year. The policy, however, required that at the beginning of the year the chiefs on each shift would reassign everyone to a new crew, so they broke up our old gang.

Full Circle

I was having a cup of coffee at old Station 3 with rookie Steve Hoffman when at 7:45 a.m. we received an emergency call about a water leak in an office building on Cannon Drive. Leonard, the captain going off shift, was a lawyer on his off time, and he was supposed to be in court at 8:30. He was very upset that his relief, Captain Davis, who was my captain was not there. Capt. Davis usually would arrive at about 7 a.m.

Steve Hoffman and I suited up and jumped on the back tail board where we rode in those days. Engineer Ellingson got in behind the wheel and Capt. Leonard was steaming as he put his helmet and coat on. He slammed the door so hard I thought it was going to fall off its hinges. Steve and I were glad we were riding on the tail board and didn't have to listen to him.

We arrived on scene, and the captain called for the toolbox and a small ladder. Steve and I went into the office building where we saw a large water leak in the ceiling of the hallway just off of the lobby. The captain instructed me to crawl up through a ceiling crawlspace opening and check for a water valve. I could tell he was still mad by the tone of his voice.

I found a water valve about ten feet away and shut it off. He was hollering something at me, but I could not understand what he was saying through ceiling and insulation. I hollered back, "I can't understand you."

He yelled back using some profanity, and I did understand that he was telling me to shut off the water valve, which I had already done. When I got back down he was still lecturing me about my hearing. I know he was mad and was taking it out on me, and because I was a rookie I didn't dare say anything back to him.

There never was an apology, so from that day on I avoided working with him and stayed clear of him as much as possible. When we returned to the station Capt. Davis was there and they had a few words. Capt. Davis later told us he was tired of coming in at seven o'clock when Leonard would always relieve him around 7:45 or so. This one morning he came in at 7:55 a.m.

Capt. Leonard retired a few years later and was out of my life until about 30 years later.

My mother-in-law was in a home for Alzheimer and dementia residents in the Agoura area. One day my wife, Shirley, and my son, Marc, and I were pushing my mother-in-law down the hallway to the visiting area. Along the hallway were the patient rooms. Alongside the door of each room was a little glass case with a couple of shelves in it. The patients had things they were familiar with placed in there so they could recognize their room.

As we were making our way down the hallway, my son said, "Hey, Dad, there is a Beverly Hills fireman here."

I said, "You're kidding."

"No. There is a Beverly Hills fire hat in this one display cabinet."

I saw Leonard's name and told my son, "You remember the story I told you about the one guy on the department that I did not get along with?"

"Yes."

"This is that guy."

We got to the visiting area, and I left my mother-in-law and wife there. My son and I went back to the room, and I knocked on the door. A voice inside said, "Come in." I opened the door and there were two gentlemen sitting there, one short and skinny, and the other one on the heavy side. I asked who Leonard was, and the heavyset gentleman said, "I am." I told him who I was, but he did not remember me. Through our conversation he did remember a couple of chiefs that he had worked for and that was about it. He was a completely different person. We talked for a while.

Every time after that when I visited my mother-in-law, Leonard and I would see each other. We would wave and sometimes visit. I was glad I got a chance to meet him again, and because he had changed so much we were friends on a different level.

A few months later I didn't see him and asked the nurse if he were still there. She said his son had taken him to Hawaii where he lived, and Leonard was now in a nursing home there. It wasn't long after that I had heard Leonard had passed away. I was sorry to hear that and was glad I had a second chance to know him. It's strange how some things in life go full circle.

First Bomb Scare

I was working at old Station 3 one afternoon when we went on our first bomb scare call. Capt. Sanchez, acting Engineer Duke Ellingson, Fireman Craig Tatro and I pulled up in front of a 12-story office building on Wilshire.

The captain, Craig and I got off the engine and went into the building. I asked the captain, "What do we look for?"

He said, "Hell, I don't know. I guess anything out of place or suspicious." He told me and Craig to go to the roof and start down, and he would go to the underground parking and start up until we met.

Craig and I made our way to the roof and opened a steel door going into a large air-conditioning room. Big fans with a lot of suction were running, so as we made our way through this large door that was left open the door was sucked in and closed with a tremendous bang. Craig and I must have jumped three feet into the air. We thought we had found the bomb. When we hit the ground and our hearts started beating again we looked at each other and laughed, because our eyes were wide open, and our faces were as white as sheets.

We made our way down to Capt. Sanchez. We found nothing, and neither did he. We told him of our experience on the roof and he had a good laugh.

We did not realize it at the time, but from then on bomb scare calls would become pretty regular. Because of the ever-changing world conditions, we would have many classes on how to handle this type of emergency from then on. Most bomb calls were false and very disruptive to the businesses in the buildings. But on a few calls we found some things that were very suspicious, and we had to call the LA bomb squad in to take care of the situation.

I talked to Craig recently, and we still laughed about it and remembered it like it was yesterday.

Gas Attack at the Beverly Wilshire

I was standing in line for lunch at the old headquarters station when Bob Jeffries came walking up behind me and said, "Slater, I have a funny story to tell you. I was inspecting the Beverly Wilshire Hotel this morning. I took the elevator up to the penthouse and on the way up I experienced this gas attack. It was bad. It shook the elevator. About that time the elevator doors opened at the penthouse and standing there were two older ladies maybe in their 80's. Dressed like they were going to high tea, they wore long, flowery, silk dresses and big, wide-brimmed hats, and white gloves," said Bob.

"I said, 'Good morning, ladies,' and stepped out of the elevator. They said, 'Good morning, sir' and stepped into the elevator. As the elevator door closed I heard one lady say to the other, 'My God, what the hell died in here?' The other lady said, 'I don't know, but it's enough to choke a frigging maggot.'"

"That was such a funny scene hearing those dignified old ladies talking like crusty old sailors I started to laugh uncontrollably. I could not stop. If anyone had seen me carrying on like that they would have thought I was having a fit," said Bob.

And with that everyone in the chow line was splitting a gut laughing. Bob was a funny guy. He would do anything for a laugh and was fun to be around. I remember coming to work a few years later the day after Halloween, and as I approached headquarters station on my way to the parking lot I saw up in front of me crossing the street going to the station this tall blonde-haired buxom lady of the night with a short miniskirt and high heels. As I got closer she turned and had a mustache. It was Bob. He smiled and waved, and I started to laugh. I thought to myself *I wouldn't be caught dead in an outfit like that.*

I parked the car, and as I was crossing the street to enter the station I heard this loud roar of laughter coming from the upstairs dining room. When I got up there Bob was prancing around and had everyone rolling on the floor with laughter.

Bob was a little nutty sometimes, but I will say this: If I had to go into a tough and dangerous situation and could only take one fireman with me, Bob would be my number one pick, because he would be up for anything, would watch my back and never let me down regardless of the circumstances. That is the highest compliment one fireman can pay to another fireman. When I confirmed this story with him, Bob said he always felt the same way about me. That made me proud.

Bob is retired now because of a lung problem. That's another story. He is living up in Cottonwood, Arizona, and I am sure he is still doing funny things and making people laugh. He was my good friend, and I always enjoyed working with him.

Third and Palm Fire

One evening around 9 p.m. I was watching television with my wife, Shirley, in our apartment located near Third and Sherbourne Drive just a few blocks out of Beverly Hills. We heard a fire engine with red lights flashing and siren blaring go by west on Third Street. Twenty seconds later we heard two more engines going in the same direction. I thought this strange. Third Street is not a main running lane, and then when I heard another engine and a ladder truck go by I told Shirley I was going to the sundeck on the roof of our five-story apartment building to see what was going on.

On the sundeck I could see a very large orange-red plume in the air maybe 300 feet tall, and it looked very close to our headquarters station. I hustled back to our apartment and told Shirley what I had seen and that I was sure they needed help, so I was going to go there and would see her later. It turned out to be much later.

I had a hard time maneuvering through the heavy traffic of spectators that this spectacular fire was attracting. I went south a few blocks and then made my way west about ten blocks to get to headquarters where I picked up my turnouts and decided because of the heavy traffic to walk the three or so blocks to the fire which was on the corner of Third and Palm. When I arrived I saw a spectacular sight, a new five-story wood-framed apartment building which was completely framed but not yet wrapped, and it was fully involved in fire.

There were at least ten fire rigs parked on Third and the adjacent side street with engines from our Beverly Hills City, LA City, and LA County Fire Department and their crews attacking the fire from all four sides. I found out later that the captain from our first engine on scene reported multiple fires on multiple floors, which indicated an arson fire.

I reported to our chief who was in charge, and he assigned me to a 2 1/2-inch line which was protecting a small apartment building on the south side of the fire. The heat was so intense that it was threatening buildings on the south and west side of the inferno. The north and east side of the buildings were across the street and far enough away to be safe, but the engines parked in the street took some pretty good heat.

As we put up a water curtain to protect these exposures we had to keep a close eye on the fire because of falling burning wood jarred loose by the powerful hose streams trying to extinguish this fire. The Beverly Hills police had their hands full keeping people out of the area.

My good friend Fireman Bill Daley was assigned to an exposure line down a narrow alley on the west side of the fire. While protecting the structures on the west side of the alley along with Fireman Amerelle, they started to get into trouble because of intense heat, and Engineer Harvey Adair noticed and ran a 1 1/2-inch line to them to protect them.

Bill Daley suffered third-degree burns on the backs of both of his hands when his wet leather tight-fitting gloves turned into very hot steam and cooked his hands. We were issued much better gloves after this fire. Bill Daley was taken to the hospital for treatment and later would require skin grafts.

Firefighter Jeremiah Hayes also was taken to the hospital. He was at the other end of the alley protecting another structure when windows high above his head exploded from the intense heat and glass rained down on him severely cutting his hands.

We all did a good job of protecting the exposures. They were singed but nothing a good paint job wouldn't fix. Some broken windows had to be replaced. We were lucky.

We finally got a handle on the fire around midnight after wetting down a large bonfire. One of our rigs, that Harvey Adair was the engineer on, suffered some blistered paint, a first for our department.

Because I was off duty the chief assigned me to fire watch which meant I was to stay there all night with a charge line and a radio, and if there were a rekindle I was to put it out. If I had needed help I would have called headquarters. They sent me a couple of hamburgers and some coffee and water. The rest of the evening was pretty much uneventful. I stayed until about 7 a.m. when I was relieved to go home.

There was not much left of the place except for a scorched foundation. I don't know to this day if they ever caught anyone who was responsible for that fire.

First Brushfire

I had been on the department a little over a year when on a fall day we were on full alert for brush fires caused by hot Santa Anna winds blowing from the desert to the sea. We received a call from the Ventura Fire Department stating they had a large brushfire burning and requesting our help. I was instructed that we were sending two engine companies, and I would be going. This would be my first brushfire, and I was excited to be one of ten going from our department. We were also told that we would be gone for at least two days and to bring what personal gear we might need.

We packed up and left a 1/2 hour later. We would rendezvous with two engine companies from Burbank and one engine company from Glendale. The strike team concept as we know it today had not yet been conceived. We headed for Ventura County some 30 miles northwest of Beverly Hills, responding with red lights and siren the whole way. This was before earplugs were commonly used.

As we crossed into Ventura County and proceeded up this curvy country road, we passed three or four old farm houses that were in the path of the fire, and the fire was bearing down on them just minutes away. I did not see any fire personnel in the area, and I wondered why we were not stopping. Then I thought if we were going past this fire situation we must be going to something really big or more important.

We continued another five miles and met our Ventura spotter who took us to our first assignment along with Burbank and Glendale fire departments. When we arrived we saw a large fire front burning down a steep hillside coming right at us. The spotter thought we might have 15 or 20 minutes before the fire would reach the road where we were parked.

He also said we had to stop the fire at the road, because if the fire were to jump the road a subdivision a mile away would be in harm's way. We had one problem. There were no hydrants, so we were on a limited water supply. Each engine held about 500 gallons, but they did say there were water tankers in the area that would try to keep up with demand.

We would attack a 500-foot fire front, so they positioned the fire rigs about every hundred feet or so to cover the area. We laid out 1 1/2-inch hose lines to the front and rear of each engine so we could cover about 100 feet of hillside.

The sun was setting and with all of the smoke in the area it was a different type of sunset, like none I had ever seen. It was not long and the fire was on top of us and within reach of our hose streams. We hit it with everything we had, and it was going okay until we started to run out of water. What a crappy feeling. I thought we might lose the battle, but the tanker was Johnny on the spot. Engineer Doug Brockert gave us another 500 gallons to finish the job. Heavy smoke and flying embers burned my eyes even though we wore goggles and a bandanna covering our nose and mouth, which did some good by keeping the large chunks out of our lungs. I know now what the term "smoke eaters" means. It was not pleasant, but it comes with the territory.

The fire had breached the line in a few places, but the fast work of the crews in the area kept the fire in check. They said we were lucky, that the wind had died down somewhat which made our job much easier. We finished by watering the area down as much as we could, trying to extinguish most of the embers. We picked up our hose lines and the tanker topped us off. We were ready for another assignment. I think they left one engine for a while to protect against a rekindle.

The spotter took our remaining engine companies to a large ranch with an old farmhouse, two large barns and some outbuildings sitting in the mouth of a narrow canyon. It was now dark, and we were told that the way the wind was blowing they expected the fire to come down the canyon sometime late night or early morning depending on how strong the wind would get.

We could see a red glow off in the distance which lit up the night sky. Chief Jackson from our department had a meeting with the other captains to decide where to place the rigs for maximum protection of the house and the barns, and then we laid out our hose lines. At around 10 p.m. the chief and his driver, Jim Grove, were going for some fast food for everyone while we tried to get some rest, because we were going to be busy in a couple of hours. About this time the other engine joined us, and this was about the time I learned that the ranch belonged to Trini Lopez, the singer, who was not there but had a small crew of men and women taking care of the place.

The chief and his driver returned shortly with a huge box of cheeseburgers, fries and soft drinks. My buddy, Steve Hoffman, was the other fireman with me. We were so hungry we made fast work of that fast food. Stephen and I agreed it was the best cheeseburger we had ever eaten. A short time after we finished eating, the chief had bought a case of beer, and he passed one beer to each guy, which was much appreciated.

The orange glow in the distance was much larger, brighter and closer, and Steve said it was coming. We thought we might get some shuteye before it arrived. He climbed up into the hose bed to lie down, and I climbed into one of the jump seats of our engine, rolled up my brush jacket for makeshift pillow and tried to get some shuteye with some success. About two hours later the captain came by and told us to get ready, that the fire was about 1000 feet away coming down the canyon as was predicted, showering large amounts of ash on us.

When the fire got within about 500 feet of us a very strange thing happened. The wind started to change directions and got stronger, and the fire made a left-hand turn. The wind took the fire up the face of the canyon, and a half hour later it went over the top and disappeared. We were left with the edge of the fire, and when it came down within reach we were able to successfully extinguish the fire with just minor damage to some small outbuildings. It was not much fire for what we were expecting, but I guess that was a good thing, because that fire coming at us with the wind could've been a big problem.

Daylight broke, and we picked up our equipment. We were invited into the old ranch house for a Mexican breakfast. All 22 of us were able to sit at the largest table I had ever seen. The food was fantastic! Eggs, potatoes, refried beans, some type of Mexican sausage, tortillas, and plenty of coffee made a good breakfast. Chief Jackson received a call from Ventura Fire that they were releasing us to return to our cities. We thanked the ladies, and everyone involved in the breakfast packed up and headed for home.

Driving out we passed through the area that the fire had gone through, and we saw a small subdivision pretty well destroyed by the fire. I had a sick feeling, thinking, *If we only had known the fire was going to turn on us, we may have done some good if we had known the subdivision was there.* As we drove down that curvy road we saw those four farm houses that were being threatened by the fire when we drove in yesterday. They were heavily damaged, and that was another disappointment.

On the way back to Beverly Hills I had a chance to think about my first brush fire and came to the conclusion that it was bittersweet. I was glad for the experience but disappointed that we could have done more. I did not know at the time, but following all of the brush fires I would fight in the next 30 years I would always come away a little disappointed. We always did our best, but most the time we were chasing the fires. Because of some delays or poor communications we were always late getting there.

I also did not know at that time that 29 years from then I would fight the biggest brushfire of my career and have the most success of saving homes, but it would also be the fire that would retire me with a heart problem caused by being in heavy smoke for two days. That will be another story.

Angels on the Roof

At about 9 p.m. at old Stations 3 I was ending my first year on the job, and the whole crew was watching the Dodgers game. Over the speaker we heard the call for Engine 3 to respond to an address on La Cienega Blvd. Arcing and sparking on the roof was reported. This address was on the famous Restaurant Row. We responded to the address, and as we pulled up in front, we saw the site of the old Fairchild restaurant that had burned down a year and a half ago, the biggest fire in town that year.

Rebuilt under a different name, the new restaurant was about to be opened. We put a 24-foot ladder up on the north side of the building as Captain Sanchez and I, along with Fireman McElroy, climbed to the roof. The three of us looked all over that roof for about 20 minutes and saw nothing, no arcing or sparking. The captain called headquarters and asked who reported this, and the operator said the call had come in from Lawry's, the famous prime rib restaurant across the street. This restaurant hosted the Rose Bowl teams every year, and they have an eating contest called the Beef Bowl to see which team can eat the most prime rib.

The three of us were about to go down the ladder, when I noticed a red glow about the size of a golf ball on this six-inch pipe which ran from the middle of the building to the electric box at the rear of the building. As we watched the glow, it grew to about the size of a softball and then exploded and shot fireballs in all directions like a Roman candle. We hit the deck almost falling off the roof. We could hear people screaming at Lawry's restaurant across the street while waiting for valet service to deliver their car. We watched that pipe turn a brilliant electric blue going all the way to the rear of the building and up to the poll and then along all the wires going along the rear of the property line, and everything turned orange. All the insulation on the wires fell off in sparks, and then we heard a large bang at the transformer down the line creating the most spectacular fireworks I had ever seen. After we caught our breath and exchanged a couple of choice words, the captain called headquarters and requested the power company to respond as soon as possible.

We had to stand by for about 20 minutes until they arrived on scene. They looked it over and told us about 15,000 volts were carried through that pipe, and if we had touched that pipe we would have been fried right there. How the three of us crawled over that roof and did not touch that pipe is amazing! I am sure our guardian angels were looking out for us that night. After they investigated what had happened they determined that the insulation had been scraped off the wires as they were being pulled through the six-inch conduit pipe.

We escaped death that night, but you record this type of experience in your brain, and the next time you go to the roof looking for trouble, you go carefully, and you pass this experience on to your fellow firemen the next day when you critique special calls like this so they can benefit from your experience. That is how you build your safety net knowledge. Fire departments across the country learn from good and bad experiences, and this one was good with no casualties.

First Broken Leg

My wife and I had just purchased a three-quarter acre parcel of land in the Malibu Park area of Malibu. It was a beautiful lot 1/2 mile off Zuma Beach, 210 feet above the ocean with a 110-degree ocean view. We were planning on building a house there. I had some experience building a house when I was a teenager helping my dad build the house we lived in while I was going through high school in Strongsville, Ohio.

We soon found out that in order to get a loan from the bank I had to be a licensed contractor, which I was not. So Chief Cass offered to help. I worked with him on the fire department, and he also was the owner of the 24-unit apartment building where my wife and I lived. We also managed the property. Chief Cass said he would go to the bank with me and identify himself as the overseer of the job. He had a contractor's license and had built his apartment building. That is what we did, and I got a loan and started construction.

About half way through construction I was having a problem, so on my way home that evening I stopped by headquarters where Chief Cass was working as the battalion chief to discuss this problem. As we were talking he took a call about a structure fire on the east side of town. He responded, and I waited to see if the call would turn out to be a false alarm. About five minutes later I could hear over the radio that Cass had a high-rise building on fire. So I knew he would not be back anytime soon.

I decided I would go to the fire and see if he needed any extra help, so I picked up my turnout equipment and drove to the scene. He was glad to see me. The fire was on the top floor of this old seven-story office building. The chief was sending the truck crew to the roof for ventilation, and he asked me to take a 1 1/2-inch line to the roof for protection. Gary Poitner, the engineer, had the 100-foot aerial ladder in place, so I was the first one up the ladder with the hose. Jim Anderson was my backup and helped me with the hose.

As I reached the top of the aerial ladder I encountered a four-foot wall which I had to step onto and jump to the roof. It was dark, and I could not see that the roof had a 30-degree slope, so when I hit the roof, my right ankle turned and I fell to the roof in pain. I knew I either had suffered a very bad sprain or a broken ankle. Jim Anderson right behind me saw what happened. I asked him to call for the paramedics to treat me for a possible broken leg.

Paramedics Mike Smollen and Mark Pierce showed up with their equipment and splint my leg. The truck crew started ventilating the roof with a chainsaw as Mark and Mike finished splinting my leg. I noticed as I was sitting on the roof the heat was coming through my Bunker pants. That roof was pretty hot. When the truck crew opened the roof they encountered heavy smoke and fire. It was time for me to get off the roof! I threw my boot over the side and with the aid of the paramedics I hobbled down the ladder one rung at a time until I reached the ground. I heard the chief over the radio ordering everyone to evacuate the roof, which was becoming spongy. The truck company made their way down the ladder, paramedics placed me on the stretcher and into the rescue, and we headed for UCLA Hospital.

Technicians x-rayed my lower right leg and found I had a broken ankle. While they were putting a cast on my leg, which went up to just below the knee, a nurse came in and said our other rescue had just bought in three injured firemen. Joel LAFirenza, better known as "Mooch," was one of them. They were injured from flying debris when the air-conditioning unit fell through the roof. They were lucky they had not been hit by the unit. UCLA patched us all up and we made it back to the station where I somehow drove about ten blocks to my apartment. It was about 3:00 a.m., and the department had called my wife earlier to let her know where I was.

She was surprised to see me in a cast. I would not return to work for about three months. This was my first broken leg that was job-related, but it would not be my last. I also broke my leg in the last part of my rookie year snow skiing at Mammoth Mountain, which put me off work for almost six months. The broken ankle slowed the construction of my house for a while, but we were able to complete the house six months later. My wife and I gave up our apartment management role and moved into our new home, which was great! Building that house was one of the best things we ever did. In this house we raised our two children, Suzanne and Marc, and we all had a great time living the Malibu beach life.

The Potato Toss

I had been on the department about two years and was working with a new rookie, Craig Tatro, just out of rookie school. He was all charged up. We had just finished our housework at old Station 3. It was around 11 a.m. and Craig was going to be our cook for the day. Captain Sanchez, Engineer Dick Lapointe, Craig, and I climbed on the engine to go shopping for food for lunch and supper at the local grocery.

For lunch Craig was having soup and ham sandwiches, and for supper he was going to prepare baked chicken, baked potatoes, and corn along with a good salad. This was his very first time cooking, so we did not know what to expect. We got to the store, and we all helped him shop. We also talked him into ice cream for dessert. When we were finished shopping we put all the groceries up in the hose bed because at that time the two firemen rode on the back tail board holding on to a handrail. The captain and engineer were in an enclosed cab up front.

Just as we pulled in to the station, we were dispatched to a structure fire in our district. So we hurriedly grabbed the bags of groceries and put them in the kitchen refrigerator. In our haste we did not realize the four big potatoes were lying in the hose bed. They must have fallen out of the bag. We were responding with red lights flashing and siren blaring down Olympic Boulevard on our way to the fire. Craig was the hydrant man, meaning he would be hooking the valve and hose to the hydrant. That was the junior fireman's job. Then the engine would lay the 2 1/2- inch hose to the fire, and when the engineer signaled he was ready for water, he would turn the water in to the engine at the fire scene.

Craig was very excited about doing this for the first time for real, not practice. We were bouncing along on the tail board, and Craig was looking at the locus valve and going over the procedure in his mind that he had practiced many times in rookie school. As he was doing this, he noticed the four big potatoes lying in the hose bed next to the locus valve. He grabbed the potatoes one by one while holding on to the handrail and threw them over his shoulder. I saw this about the time he was throwing the last two potatoes. I asked, "What the hell are you doing?"

"I was told in rookie school to never have anything in the hose bed that may interfere with making a hydrant."

"Did you see what the hell you did to that Cadillac following us?"

"No."

"All four potatoes bounced off the hood and windshield of that big Cadillac following us."

"I'm going to hear about this."

"Don't worry. The Cadillac was following us way too close."

About this time the engine approached the hydrant, and the call was canceled. Before we returned to the station we informed the captain that we had to shop for four more potatoes because we had thrown the last four at a Cadillac for following us too close. The captain thought we were teasing him because he was fun to kid. He said, "Oh my God! I'm going to hear from the chief tonight." He was kidding us now, and when he saw the worried look on Craig's face, he laughed and said, "Kid, don't worry about it. If that Cadillac was so close you could hit it with a potato, it was following us too damn close."

We returned to the station, and Craig fixed two fine meals. There was one problem. He cooked enough for one big helping, each. Engineer Dick Lapointe was a small guy, but he could eat more than anyone on the department, and he sure complained to Craig about this. We laughed at him and Craig said, "That's called portion control."

Dick replied with a one-finger salute.

We never heard anything about the Cadillac incident. I am sure the driver never followed a fire engine that closely again. Greg Tatro left our department a few years later to work for the LA County Fire Department. He was fun to work with and was a practical joker. We have stayed good friends to this day. I recently talked to him about this story, and we had a good laugh.

The Most Comical Rescue Call

When I became a fireman for the city of Beverly Hills in 1964 there was no such thing as a paramedic program. That would happen in the early 1970's. Until then we were trained in advanced first aid. Our ambulance was a Chevy panel truck converted to an ambulance.

We would take all patients to an aid station in Beverly Hills located on the western side of the city. They had a staff of one or two doctors and a couple of nurses 24-7. On this one day I was assigned to Rescue 1 along with Chuck Alvey who would be the driver.

Mid-afternoon we responded to the Beverly Hilton Hotel on a chest pain call in the men's room. We arrived on scene and found a middle-aged man who was an off-duty security guard for the hotel sitting on the floor. He was complaining of chest pains. We could tell he had a few drinks. He had a strong Irish or Scottish accent. When we checked him out, we told him we were going to transport him to the aid station. He wanted no part of this and kept saying in his heavy accent that he was not going with us. After about 15 minutes we finally convinced him to go, but he was not happy.

About ten minutes later we arrived at the aid station, and he complained all the way. It was the booze talking.

Chuck parked in front of the station and opened the rear doors. He pulled his end of the stretcher out, and I had a good hold on the other end of the stretcher. When the stretcher cleared the back of the rig the wheels of the stretcher at his end came down and locked into place, but the wheels at my end did not come down and the head end of the stretcher fell to the ground pulling me out of the rig causing me to do a complete somersault landing in the street. I looked up at Charlie who was trying to pull the guy by his feet onto the stretcher which was at a 40-degree angle. The guy with pillow in hand threw it straight up in the air and said, "Now I am sure I'm not going with you." Chuck was looking around to see who was watching this keystone operation as I picked myself off the pavement. Charlie and I began to laugh. It was such a funny scene. We got the patient secured, and in his tipsy state and with heavy accent he expressed his feelings in so many words.

Laughing, we wheeled him up to the front door, and the nurse opened the door. We could hardly explain to her that he was possibly having a heart attack. She looked at us like we were nuts. We wheeled him in, and they took over. We later explained to the nurse what had happened, and she had a good laugh. By the time we left the patient was stabilized, and we were his best friends. I think doctors determined he had a bad case of indigestion.

For weeks after that every time I thought about that call I would start to smile and sometimes laugh, and sometimes in public people would look at me strangely. That was the funniest scene I had in my 30-year career.

Peas and Corn

*J*im Hodges and Marv Johnson were on Rescue 1 one afternoon, and between calls they were playing pool at the old Headquarter Station. The pool table was located at the far end of a large dining room across from the kitchen. The cook for the day, Bob Marshall, was making supper until he was dispatched with the truck company to a flooding call. On his way out of the dining room he asked Jim and Marv to watch the food while they were playing pool.

They were so engrossed in the game they forgot until they smelled something burning and smoke coming out of the kitchen. They ran into the kitchen to find the pot of peas burned to a crisp. Jim and Marv looked all over the kitchen, and lucky for them they found four cans of corn. They cleaned out the peas, put in corn on a slow simmer, threw the corn cans out and left the pea cans on the counter. They were tricksters and were playing a joke on Bob. Then they went back to playing pool.

When Bob returned about a half hour later, he went into the kitchen and noticed the corn. He looked at the peas can then looked at the corn in the pot. He scratched his head and looked puzzled. Then he took another look at the peas can and then the corn. I came into the dining room at this time, and they clued me in. We all started to snicker as we watched Bob contemplate the situation.

Then he heard us laughing, picked up a broom and said, "You SOB," and chased all of us out of the dining room and down the stairs to the apparatus floor with much laughter on our part. Bob would not ask Marv or Jim to watch anything again.

When supper time came he put out a nice meal of fried chicken, mashed potatoes and gravy, corn, and a large salad. The guys were all clued in by this time and kept asking Bob where the hell are the peas? Bob's firehouse humor responded by giving us the one-finger salute as we continued laughing.

Bob was killed along with three other firemen and a pilot about a year later in a plane crash while returning home from a hunting trip. That was a very sad time for our department, and that is another story. Bob was a good fireman, very quiet, and pleasant to be around.

Cat in a Tree

I remember working at old Station 3 one day with Capt. Al Sanchez. He was a fun guy to work with, but this morning he received a call from the chief to get a cat out of a tree. He was not happy about this and was grumbling as we climbed aboard and turned on the red lights and siren. About halfway there a car pulled out in front of us, and we damn near T-boned him. This really made Cappy mad. By the time we arrived on scene he was boiling. The lady owner of the cat was at the curb when we pulled up. The captain opened the door, stepped out and in a loud voice asked the lady how many dead cat skeletons she had seen in a tree. She said none, and Al said. "That's my point." With all the commotion at the base of the tree the cat came halfway down, made a great leap, hit the center of the yard and took off like a bat out of hell around the corner of the house never to be seen again, at least not by us.

After that I was a firm believer in what goes up will come down, until several years later I was working at old headquarters. I was in the watch office when a guy called in saying his four-year-old daughter's cat was up a tree and she had been crying for about three hours. The chief on duty turned him down and told him to call the animal control office.

The next day I was working overtime, which I would do a lot. The same father called in now pleading with another chief that his daughter had been crying for two days and the cat had not budged, so the chief said okay. They dispatched the truck on which I was the tillerman who steered the back of the truck. We arrived on scene and this cat was at the top of a 60-foot tree. Engineer Poitner laid the 100-foot aerial ladder up into the tree. George Richards and I were told to get that cat down, and I told George to go first.

He said, "Why me?"

I said, "I am senior, and besides, you're going for Engineer soon, and a cat rescue will look really good on your portfolio. I will do a good job backing you up."

He said sarcastically, "Thanks, Slater." Then we proceeded to climb to the top of the ladder.

George grabbed for the cat and missed. The cat was hungry, scared and mad. George made a second try and got a good, firm grip on the cat which proceeded to scratch, bite, and urinate all over him. George turned around and in a smart voice as I was laughing said, "Thanks, Slater. I needed this."

I said, "You will get the job for sure now, George." We then climbed down the ladder. George handed the cat to the little girl, and she looked at George like he was Superman.

Later, I said to George, "Did you see the look on that little girl's face? She will remember you for the rest of her life. Now, wasn't that worth it?"

George replied, "I guess so, but I am still mad at you." He then chased me around the apparatus floor. A few months later George was promoted to Engineer, and he probably never had to climb another ladder.

Gas Spill at the Beverly Wilshire

I was off duty this particular day, and the story was told to me by Fireman Tom Crewse on my return to work the next shift. This was probably the most hazardous situation the department had ever confronted involving almost the entire on-duty shift of 23 personnel made up of four engine companies and a truck company, the chief and his driver, the fire marshal and two fire inspectors.

If things had gone south, the entire 23 personnel would've been gone in a flash. It was mid-morning when a gas tanker parked on a side street on the west side of the Beverly Wilshire Hotel was pumping gas to some pumps located on the first sub-terrain garage area.

The problem was that the driver was new and had hooked up to an old storage tank that was disconnected. Hundreds of gallons of gas had spilled out onto the underground parking area before he realized the problem.

When the chief arrived with all of the rigs and personnel, he was faced with all kinds of problems. He had to stop all hotel guests from coming into the area, shut down all sources of ignition, and get the gas and fumes out as quickly as possible in a hotel that was pretty well filled to capacity. The chief called for a special truck with the capacity to pump the gas out of the building, but until that truck arrived, firefighters used buckets and barrels filling them by using metal shovels. Realizing they could cause a spark by scraping along the concrete, they switched to bleach bottles with the bottoms cut off and used the handle of the bottle to create an excellent scoop.

At one point Tom said some guy got past the barriers and attempted to start his car. Every firefighter's heart stopped for about five seconds, and they all screamed at him. The poor guy probably still can't hear. Tom said that fumes were terrible and the guys had to take turns going out for fresh air.

The pumper truck arrived, which seemed an eternity, and then the operation went much faster even though the whole shift was in that hazardous situation for over three hours. Everything went well. I do believe they had some help from above to protect them and everyone in the hotel that day.

In the following days many critiques were shared on what went right and what they did wrong, because the department had never before run into a gas spill situation of this magnitude. One officer was so troubled by what could have happened he decided he never again wanted to be in a position to put that many people in harm's way, and he decided to finish his career in the fire prevention bureau. After that incident I was told all gas pumps in the sub-parking areas were taken out of service. Tom Crewse years later became battalion chief.

Back from Death, Thanks to Moses

Our fire department was the fifth department in the world to have certified paramedics. LA County, LA City, Englewood, California; Miami, Florida; and Beverly Hills were the first five. Every firefighter on our department had to go through Emergency Medical Technician (EMT) certification.

One evening at new Station 3 at about 8 p.m. we received our first full cardiac arrest call after completing our training. The call was to the new Academy Award Theater located in our district. The call came in as a full arrest. We responded to a packed theater for a private showing of *One Flew over the Cuckoo's Nest* starring Jack Nickolson. The showing was for all Hollywood stars and producers. Rescue 1 arrived at the same time we did. We all got our equipment and went into the lobby. The manager directed us down this one aisle. The lights were on, and as we hurried down the aisle we could see a man on his back crosswise in the aisle and two people were working on him.

As we got closer I saw Charlton Heston ("Moses") doing chest compressions. We found out later the other man was a doctor who was doing mouth to mouth. They stepped aside, and we went into full operation. The man was 60 years old and had no pulse. He was not breathing, so I started chest compressions. Chuck Beagle ventilated. Mark Pierce and Tommy Cass were the two paramedics. One established contact with UCLA Hospital, and the other hooked up the monitor and started the IV. The lights were on. The thing that seemed so strange was the theater was so quiet you could hear a pin drop. The only sounds we heard were the doctor at UCLA talking to Mark Pierce who was on the radio. After about 15 minutes of doing all the things we had been taught, I began to feel a pulse in my palm as I did the compression. I said, "I think we have a pulse."

Tom said, "Stop compressions and let's look." Sure enough we had a good pulse. About a minute later the man took a breath. As his chest rose Mark informed the doctor who told us to bring him in, that we had done a good job.

At that point the whole theater audience stood up and cheered, giving us a standing ovation. I was never so proud and embarrassed at the same time. I could not wait to get out of there. We loaded him on the gurney, assisted his breathing, and headed up the aisle to make our run to the UCLA emergency room. He was doing fine.

About two weeks later he walked out of the hospital. We returned to headquarters after we left UCLA to tell the guys what had happened, because this was our very first arrest, and our patient had straight-lined and returned to life. We had seen it happen. The techniques we all learned worked, and after we told the whole story, one fireman in the back said, "Hell, that's nothing. Anyone who had Moses pumping on their chest would survive." Everyone laughed. It was a special moment for all of us. That was a save, so I painted a Roman numeral One in yellow on my helmet. Before my career was finished I would put 14 more marks on my helmet.

Chief Daley sent Charlton Heston a commendation for getting involved. Charlton Heston, who had played Moses in the film *The Ten Commandments*, and the doctor at the theater had kept the man alive until we arrived, providing what is needed for success, people at the scene getting involved. Everyone should learn CPR. We have only six minutes to start CPR, and if we can't get there in that time the patient most likely will not survive.

When I tell this story to the old-timers they get the Charlton Heston Moses connection, but if I tell this story to young people, they don't get it, because the more recent depiction of Moses is by another actor, not Heston.

This story tells the first cardiac save that I was a part of. I eventually would be involved in 15 saves that I marked on my helmet

Tea for the Tillerman

I arrived at old headquarters station early one morning, changed into my uniform and joined the gang in the dining room for coffee. The main topic of conversation was a Detroit tillerman who was decapitated the day before when the door came down on him as they drove the truck out of the station responding to a fire. I was interested in this because I was the tillerman on the A shift. Chief Tarquinio was involved in the conversation, and I heard him say that could happen here very easily. He said he could put a roll cage over the tillerman's compartment which now consisted of a flimsy windshield, steering wheel and a seat providing no protection at all.

So that morning Chief Tarquinio and Hank Bender, the shop mechanic, went to the drawing board and started designing a roll cage. Next shift they started fabricating it, and three shifts later it was finished. It sure looked good. They even installed a roof panel to keep their tillerman somewhat out of the sun and rain.

Six months later I was working at headquarters where I was the tillerman. I made myself a cup of tea. My wife had been after me to try green tea instead of coffee, so I did. I was about halfway through the cup when the truck was dispatched to the House of Suede at Wilshire and Santa Monica.

The cops thought they had a burglar on the roof and needed a tall ladder.

I slid down the poll, got into my turnouts, and climbed into the tiller seat. When the cab of the truck cleared the door, the watch office operator closed the door. The door came down and it was on the aerial ladder rails which were 18 inches below my neck and closing at 20 mph. I thought, "Oh, crap! We are going to see if this cage is going to work." Then we blew through the door which was wrapped around the cage, and as we made a left-hand turn the door rolled off to the right and bounced onto the curb and sidewalk. It almost landed in the moat that went around the library across the street. Drivers of the three cars that stopped for us as we exited the station must have wondered what the hell was going on.

The cage worked perfectly. There was no harm to me or the cage. We had no radio communication in those days. Everything looked okay except for the door, so I decided not to signal by a horn to stop, and so we continued on with the call.

When we arrived on scene I asked the engineer, Bob Robinson, if he had seen what he had done to the door.

He said, "What door?"

I said, "You took out the station door."

He proceeded to tell me how full of crap I was. Bob then positioned the aerial ladder, and the cops checked out the roof. After about one hour the cops decided their burglar suspect was gone. We returned to headquarters, and as we pulled up front we could see that the door we took out had been fixed. We backed in, dismounted, and Bob said, "Slater, what kind of BS story were you telling me?"

I said I wasn't dreaming and asked him to go out in the drill yard with me and take a look. So we did, and there next to the building was a door all mangled. Bob said, "I'll be damned."

The reason the door was fixed so fast was that the door company was working on another door 50 feet away, and they had all the material to fix it. I would have liked to have seen their reaction when they heard the door being torn out and dumped on the far side of the street. They must have thought *These guys are tough on doors.*

I said, "Bob, I got to go thank a chief for saving my life."

The policy on who opens and closes the door for the truck changed that day, and that is why the tillerman to this day is the one who opens and closes the door. As far as I know they never had another problem, but I'll tell you it was spooky, and when I went up to the dining room that day, I dumped out the tea and never drank another cup of tea at work. I am not superstitious or anything.

Lyle Slater seated at the tillerman's wheel before the protective cage was installed

LYLE SLATER

Lyle Slater standing on the truck next to the protective cage

Angels in the Night

I was working at the old headquarters station and was riding Engine 1 when at about 2 a.m. I was sound asleep in this large dormitory with about 14 other firemen when the lights came on and bells started banging. It was a general alarm over the PA system. The voice announced a structure fire on Rexford Drive about two blocks south of the station. We all jumped into our boots and Bunker pants and slid the fire pole down to the apparatus floor and mounted our rigs.

As we pulled out of the station, we could smell smoke and see a large plume up between the trees in the night sky. We stopped in front of single-story house fully involved in fire. In Beverly Hills when there is a structure fire anywhere in town all three stations get involved. They all lay lines in from different hydrants and attack the fire. The truck company went to the roof to ventilate, and after about an hour of hard work we had it pretty well extinguished except a pocket of fire down a long hallway in the rear of the house.

I took a hose line through a sliding glass door and LaFouge, a rookie, came along to back me up. Just before we were finished my air tank bell went off meaning I had five minutes of air left to get out. They teach in rookie school that when that bell goes off, you start to back out immediately.

The rookie said, "Lyle, your air tank bell is ringing!"

Over the years of going to fires you learn how much you can push the envelope. But what saved our lives here was the fact I wanted to enforce what they say in rookie school to take the training very seriously.

I said, "Let's back out now." As we reached the large, broken glass door, the rookie stepped out. As I was backing out I had one foot out of the structure and one foot in. I heard a large cracking noise, and Capt. Bruce Mauer who was standing just outside of the structure grabbed my arm and pulled me out as the whole roof came crashing down and knocked the nozzle out of my hand. A big cloud of dust, smoke and flying embers hit us in our face masks. Where we had been standing a second ago there were a couple of tons of plaster wall and roofing material.

The rookie said, "Crap! This is a dangerous job."

I said, "When you get your paycheck, you have always more than earned it, Ed."

Years later when I retired the rookie became a battalion chief, and when I would visit the station when he would be on duty, we would recall that story. The new guys would get a kick out of it. Someone definitely was looking out for us that night.

Recently, I received the sad news that Ed LaFouge had passed away from complications from leukemia and pneumonia. He was a good friend and firefighter.

One in a 1 Million Chance

It was 6 a.m. when I was leaving for work on an October morning in Malibu. As I opened the front door, a blast of hot air hit me in the face with a 50 mph wind behind it. This was a strong Santa Ana wind. I thought to myself, *We might be in trouble here in Malibu today.*

As I drove down the coast highway the gusts of wind were blowing the car all over the road. One hour later I arrived at old headquarters station in Beverly Hills. At about 10 a.m. my wife, Shirley, called to say she had seen smoke coming from the Agoura area. I did not know about this, and I told her I would check in with the watch office to see if they had any news of a brush fire burning in that area.

I found out that a brush fire was burning in Agoura just south of the 101 freeway. I called my wife back and told her to get into brush fire mode, meaning get the house, yard, and outside animals ready for fire. I told her to keep an eye on it but not to worry, because it was 15 miles away.

I did not know then that this fire would be the fastest moving fire on record. Around noon LA County Fire called for assistance, and we went into strike team mode at this time. Our strike team was made up of two engine companies from Beverly Hills, two engine companies from Santa Monica, and one engine company from Long Beach some 35 miles away, and also a chief and his driver from one of the departments that rotated after each incident. In this case it would be a Long Beach chief and his driver.

On our department the two engine companies would be assigned to go with eight men on board, so these positions had to be filled before departing to avoid leaving Beverly Hills unprotected. The duty captain with help started calling off-duty personnel to fill the void, and when all off-duty personnel had arrived, the strike team headed for the Santa Monica station, because that was in the direction we would be going to Malibu.

And then all five engine companies and the Long Beach chief and driver would leave for Malibu, because that is where the wind was driving the fire. As we waited at Santa Monica my wife called. Our department had told her we were at Santa Monica station. This was before anyone knew about a cell phone, so when she called me at Santa Monica, she told me she took our three-year-old daughter, Suzanne, to her grandparents' house in Inglewood 30 miles away. She said when she left our house the smoke was coming over our house, and she thought the fire was not far behind.

We waited for an hour at Santa Monica. Long Beach had not shown up. We were getting reports on the radio that the fire was about to jump the coast highway in the Point Dume and Malibu Park area of Malibu, which was my neighborhood. I told Capt. Mauer, "Let's get the hell out of here!"

He said, "We have to wait for the strike team leader from Long Beach."

"That's bull crap. Four engines would be better than none." I was growing impatient.

About 20 minutes later, Long Beach finally showed up. They had gotten caught in heavy rush-hour traffic. I could not figure out what brain surgeon teamed us up with a

DIVINE THUMP

department so far away when you are always in a hurry in a situation like this.

After a few minutes with red lights flashing and siren blaring we hit the road for Malibu Park some 20 miles away. In 20 minutes we were in the Point Dume area, and as we made our way down the coast highway we could look over into Malibu Park, my neighborhood. Bill Lucas, the other fireman, and I looked toward my house and the home I had built next door with two other firemen buddies. Bill said, "It doesn't look good, Slater."

Smoke was so heavy in the area of my house I could not tell if it were trees or my house that was burning. We turned off the coast highway onto Bush Drive and stopped there for our spotter. This was the road my house was on. I dismounted and ran up to the chief and told him I lived on this street and asked if we could check out my house. He said we have to go where the spotter takes us, so we headed up the hill toward my house.

Two minutes later our chief radioed back and said the last engine company in line dropped off at the corner of Bush and Merritt Drive and took the hydrant there. I could not believe it. That was on the corner where I lived. Just before we got there I could see enough through the heavy smoke that both houses were still standing and not on fire, but most of the trees around the houses were in flames.

We were the last engine company in line, so we took that hydrant 100 feet from my front door. Engineer Al Kozak drove the engine toward my house laying a 2 1/2 inch hose. He stopped between my house and my neighbor's, next door. Bill Lucas said, "Slater, take your house. I will take your neighbor's house." So Capt. Mauer, Bill, and I went into action. I could not believe this was a one in 1 million chance after all the fires burning in California at this time, and they changed our orders a couple times as we traveled to the fire

81

area, that I would end up fighting a fire at my house. Unbelievable! It was like someone was guiding me home.

The wind was so strong that the hose stream under high pressure would go out about ten feet and make a right-hand turn. I had to get upwind to have a chance to extinguish the fire. I was able to knock down most of the fire in the large eucalyptus trees bordering my house and my neighbor's. I was also able to extinguish some fires in some outbuildings and cages we had for birds, but they did sustain some damage. The house was in good shape. It was stucco and had a Class A roof and no brush within 100 feet of the structures.

Bill had pretty good luck with my neighbor's house which had wood siding but a good roof and brush clearance, except for the trees. He did lose some outbuildings. The house I had built on speculation was holding up well, and other than the trees and small bushes that burned, it was okay. As we had things pretty well under control at my house, I looked across the street to the east of me. My neighbor about 500 feet away was building a house. That property appeared to be on fire. We picked up our equipment and headed over there, but on arrival we saw it was his large lumber pile that was on fire, so we went to work on that.

As we were working on that my neighbor showed up to help. He said he was up at the shopping center above Malibu Park where everyone was evacuated to, and he could see our flashing red lights in his area, so he decided to come to help. I am glad he did. We needed the help. At first because of the smoke he did not realize he was talking with his neighbor. He was surprised when he recognized me. We got his lumber pile under control to the point where he could handle it with his garden hose, and we took off to roam the neighborhood doing what we could to assist residents and other fire personnel in the area. Some homes were destroyed, and that disturbed me because of all the time wasted waiting for Long

Beach. I think we could have done some good there had we arrived an hour and a half earlier.

As we headed down to the command post we passed my house. I said, "Let's stop. I have some cold beverages in the refrigerator." I wanted to check for a rekindle. When I entered the house, I was surprised to see my wife and her father, and she about fell over when she saw me. She said she and her dad watched from the shopping center and thought we had lost everything. I told her I had fought the fire at our house, and she was surprised. I told her I was getting some cold drinks and had to leave. She said she had a story to tell when I get home. I told her I had a story to tell her. I gave her a kiss and said, "Thanks, Pop, for helping." Then I left.

The next morning I arrived at home and my father-in-law was still there with my wife. They had stood fire guard all night. They told me their story. My wife said they had returned to our house about the time the fire hit. They were able to get all of the birds she had been rescuing in Malibu out of the cages. The fire and smoke was getting so bad that she thought our spec. house was on fire, but the fire she was looking at was a reflection of the fire in the trees on the large glass windows we had installed.

She was able to get all the birds into carrying cases and into her car, and she headed for the beach 1/2 mile away. She said she had to drive through fire twice to get there. Then she made her way up to the shopping center where all the residents for Malibu Park had been evacuated to. I told her that's about the time we had arrived in Malibu Park. She said while they were at the shopping center someone in the crowd said, "That looks like Slater's house on fire." So later she returned with her dad, and they were both surprised to see both houses standing. That was quite a night for all of us. We thanked God for the outcome. I am sure He was with us.

I was still upset about the delay in our response while waiting for the Long Beach strike team to arrive. I had to wait two days before they repaired the phone lines in our area, and when they did I called the chief who was in command of the fire. After about two hours of getting the runaround, I finally got to talk to him. I explained I was a fireman from Beverly Hills who was dispatched to Malibu to fight the fire, and also that I was a resident. I told him we were an hour and a half late getting to Malibu, because we had to wait for a chief and an Engine company which was located in Long Beach while my neighborhood was on fire. I expressed how irritated and frustrated I was about the whole situation. I said that made no sense. He said a lot of strike teams were late, and that they will have to reorganize that system.

About a week later, city officials held a meeting with the fire department and the residents of Malibu. The residents were not happy. Residents were unhappy because strike teams had to wait for orders that were late in coming while people were screaming for help. Strike teams were unfamiliar with the area, and they could see things burning but did not know how to get to the fires. They must have not had any spotters familiar with the area. Everyone was not on the same frequency. The meeting was good, because it brought out all of the problems the fire service had, and because of that bad experience for Malibu, they were able to correct most of the problems.

In our case our new strike team was made up of two engine companies from Beverly Hills, two from Santa Monica, and one from Culver City. All of these cities are in the same area, and in the future brushfires we responded to I saw a big improvement in firefighting efficiency.

Three A.M. Office Call

I was sound asleep at the old headquarters station, sleeping in this large dormitory with 14 other firemen when the lights came on, bells started banging and over the speaker blasted the dispatcher's voice: "High-rise fire on Wilshire Boulevard."

We all jumped up and into our boots next to our beds. I pulled up my Bunker pants which were folded down over our knee-high boots, grabbed my shirt and headed for the fire pole. I checked the clock. It was 3 a.m. I hit the pole, slid down to the apparatus floor next to Engine 1 which I was riding on this shift. I climbed aboard, got into my seat, slid into my air tank, put my helmet on, and out the door we went following the chief's car. Engine 5 and Engine 6 along with the truck followed us.

We turned right onto Wilshire Boulevard and headed west about five blocks and pulled up in front of this 12-story high-rise office building. The captain called for a small ladder to get the keys out of the Knox Box, a small black box above the front entrance which contains all the keys for the building. Then Neil Renfro, the other fireman, and I along with the captain grabbed all of the equipment, hose, pack lantern, ax, and sledgehammer, and went to the lobby security desk.

The security guard informed us according to the fire panel that there was a fire on the 10th floor, so we hit the stairwell and started our climb. The hardest thing a fireman must do is climb stairs with gear, in this case 10 stories carrying over 100 pounds of equipment. You cannot take the elevators, because they could malfunction in a fire situation and dump you off at the fire floor. So we climbed. It always seemed that the fires were on the upper floors, very seldom on the first floor. The other companies were a few floors behind us. We made it to the 10th floor pretty winded. This is why firemen have to work out, to stay in shape at any age because one minute you're sound asleep flat on your back, and five minutes later your heart is pounding so hard it feels like it's going to pound itself right out of your chest after a 10 or 12-story climb. I don't know how they do it in New York with so many high-rise buildings to climb. We caught our breath for a few seconds, put on air masks, and turned on our air tanks just as we were joined by Engine 5.

We opened the fire door and encountered light smoke. As we moved farther down the hallway, smoke got thicker, and we began to feel doors. We encountered two doors about 50 feet apart that were hot to the touch, so we hooked up our hose lines. Engine 5 had three guys on one door with Andy Volisky on the nozzle. I had the other nozzle at the other door. The captain unlocked both doors, and I signaled that I was ready to go in. Neil Renfro was backing me up. We opened the door slowly, staying to the side and encountered smoke and flames in our faces. I turned on the nozzle, setting it at a semi-fog. We hit the fire and crawled on our hands and knees. I could hear glass crashing. I thought it was ceiling lights and everything being knocked off the desks.

The smoke was so thick that visibility was zero as Neil and I worked our way in slowly. We ran into a large desk and started to make our way around the desk. We hesitated for a couple of seconds, then through the smoke we could see star-like images as more smoke cleared. Neil and I could see the star-like images of city lights 10 stories below. Then as more smoke cleared we could see that all of the windows from floor to ceiling were broken out! That was the breaking glass we had heard. It's a good thing we had hesitated and had not crawled through that smoke, because we would have crawled right out of that 10-story floor! I hollered as loud as I could through my mask that the windows were out and to be careful.

That is how firemen get killed, running into something unexpected. I had never encountered this situation where the windows were completely gone. The experience would be etched in my mind, forever. Someone was watching over us that night.

We were able to extinguish the fire fairly easily with two hose lines from two different directions, and then we had to overhaul it. Overhauling is going through the entire office and making sure all the sparks and embers were extinguished to avoid having to fight the fire, again. That would be unprofessional and embarrassing. After a couple of hours we picked up our equipment and returned to the station. About that time the sun was starting to rise. I had a cup of coffee with the guys and had a story to tell the oncoming shift.

I took a shower and headed home. For weeks after that I would think about that night in the high-rise without windows. The thoughts would give me chills.

I recently contacted Neil Renfro to confirm this story. We both have been retired for some 18 years at this writing. He lives in Oregon with his wife. I asked him if he remembered that fire.

"Like it was yesterday," he said.

I asked, "Do you remember how we hesitated for a minute?"

"Yes, it was a good thing, or we would not be talking to each other, now."

"Why do you think we hesitated?"

"I think we had angels on our shoulders."

"I'm glad you said that, because that's exactly how I feel."

Gene Kelly Fire

It was about a week before Christmas, and I was working at the old headquarters tillering the truck. About 8 p.m. we received a call from our paramedics requesting Truck 4 and the Jaws of Life to cut out a deceased person who wrapped his car around a tree. The car was stolen, and he had been running from the cops when he lost control on Coldwater Canyon Boulevard. We were responding up Coldwater Canyon and were almost on scene when we received another call to a structure fire. We were ordered to turn around and respond to the fire a little southwest from our location.

We went back down Coldwater to Sunset, turned west and drove a few blocks and turned south. As we made the turn halfway down the block, we could see a red glow and sparks flying over the trees on the west side of the street. As we pulled up in front of the house, we saw a man very frustrated and angry.

The man turned out to be Gene Kelly. He was mad because he had heard us coming, and when we turned north to go to the car wreck he thought we didn't know where we were going. He relayed this concern to the captain.

Mr. Kelly knew that his daughter had called the fire department, but what he didn't know was his daughter said we had a fire and hung up without providing an address. This was before 911 was set up to automatically give the address, so there was a delay before a neighbor across the street from the fire called it in with an address. That second call is why the truck was on scene first because we were very close.

The house was pretty well involved with fire coming out of most of the windows in front of the house on the first floor. We took a ladder off the truck and placed it so we could get to the roof to ventilate if needed. By this time we could hear the rest of the fire rigs coming about a mile away. About two minutes later they pulled up front with the water supply and we went into fire attack mode. Engine 1 took a line through the front door, and Engine 5 attacked the fire through a large window in front. They also took a 2 1/2-inch hose to the rear of the house and split it off to 2 1/2 lines. I ended up on one of the lines. Chuck Beagle, the engineer on Engine 5, turned the water into my line, and I took the line in through the back door. I encountered heavy smoke and heat as I crawled down this hallway with Chuck Oseguera backing me up. I could see through the smoke the orange glow and could hear the fire crackling. I turned the nozzle on and attacked the fire. I could tell at least one fire crew was inside, because every once in a while I would get hit with spray from their hose line.

We worked on that fire quite a while before we had it extinguished, and the overhaul took quite a while because of the extensive fire damage. We could have probably saved more of the house had there not been a delay because of the lack of address from the first caller.

I heard a rescue pull up, and I found out later that Frank Salcido had fallen through a glass shower door while trying to get into the attic and severely cut his wrist. He was transported to UCLA where doctors said that if the cut had been any deeper he may have lost movement in his hand, which could have been job threatening.

The story we were told by Gene Kelly was that the large Christmas tree located near the stairway caught on fire blocking him and his family who were on the second floor from exiting that way. They were lucky enough to exit the second floor a different way. We were told that Gene Kelly lost a lot of memorabilia and a large hat collection that he had acquired over the years. The house was pretty well destroyed, and at one point the chief explained to Mr. Kelly why there was a delay. I guess he understood.

About three or four years later, Engine 1 which I was on that day responded with Rescue 1 to his house because their maid was having chest pains, and I was surprised to see the house was built back the way it had looked before the fire, a new, old house. The maid was taken to the hospital for evaluation, from what I remember.

Beverly Hills Drug Bust

I was working at the old headquarters station on Engine 1 at about 5 p.m., running around the perimeter of the apparatus floor which was part of my workout when I heard a muffled explosion that made the hair on my head stand up. *What the hell was that?* I found out about 30 seconds later when the dispatcher came over the intercom and said we had a house explosion and fire northeast of the station about a mile away.

Gary Poitner, engineer on Engine 1, was the first one down the pole. I jumped into my turnouts, boots, and Bunker pants, put my coat and helmet on, climbed aboard, slid into my air tank, and out the door we went red lights flashing and siren blasting.

We arrived on scene a couple minutes later to see a house partially blown off its foundation and the front door blown off. We could see into the house and down the hallway which was on fire. We took a 1 1/2-inch line in through the front door and extinguished the fire in the hallway and also in a bathroom to the left. It was not much of a fire, and we had it extinguished in a couple of minutes. Later, we found out we were lucky.

We started looking around the house and found thousands of dollars in bundles of $100 bills lying all over the bed in one of the rear bedrooms. We also found millions of dollars of cocaine in plastic bags in the attic of this house and all types of chemicals stored in all of the closets around the house.

The LA bomb squad was called in to check the place out and take care of the chemicals. After their inspection we were told that there were enough chemicals in the house to level an entire block had the chemicals caught fire. The house was still pretty well damaged. The explosion had blown out the back of the house.

The Beverly Hills police stopped three Colombians speeding through town to UCLA Hospital for treatment of burns they had received while washing cocaine in the bathtub of this house when it blew. It's amazing they survived.

This was the biggest drug bust in California at the time. It was funny that the neighbor next door who was on vacation was the city mayor. I heard a story that he made a speech at some event declaring that there was not a drug problem in Beverly Hills. I think he may have been very surprised when returning from vacation. These days in this ever-changing world you never know what you're going to run into.

Were we lucky or what? Had that house been more involved in fire than it had been, we could have been in big trouble with all of the explosive chemicals we found. Being so close to the station, we were able to extinguish the small fire before it involved the chemicals.

LYLE SLATER

Capt. Dennis Andrews, Tillerman Lyle Slater, and Engineer George Richards

The Battle of Beverly Hills

The Shah of Iran, before he was overthrown, on occasions would come to the Los Angeles area for treatment of a serious medical condition, possibly a heart condition. While he was in the area he stayed in a large mansion. I was told that it belonged to his sister. The mansion was located in the northern part of Beverly Hills.

I was working at the old headquarters assigned to ride Engine 5 this shift. We had just finished housework, cleaning and maintaining the station and equipment, when we received a general alarm of bushes burning in our northern district. This required a full response.

When we arrived on scene we were surprised by a large crowd of about 500 Iranians who were demonstrating against the Shah and his family. They found out somehow that he was staying in this mansion.

The police department was on scene but never contacted the fire department to tell us what we were up against. This policy would change. Things were starting to get out of control. The demonstrators set fire to bushes along the street in front of the mansion. We could not reach the fire because of the large crowd that would not get out of the way.

Some of the demonstrators started taking some axes off of our truck when our engineer on the truck, Jerry Grossman, got off the rig along with the other crew members and confronted the demonstrators. Jerry ended up in a fight. You do not screw with Jerry's truck. The Beverly Hills Police Department called for backup, and when the Sheriff's Department showed up a few minutes later they got their bullhorns out and warned the crowd twice to get out of the way. The crowd did not move much, so the Sheriff drove through the crowd with some demonstrators being struck and thrown over the hoods of squad cars. That got the demonstrators' attention and we were able to get to the fire and extinguish it. Police soon were able to disperse the crowd. I had never seen anything like it. Our rescue units were called on scene to attend to the injured and transport them to the hospital.

The fire department that afternoon called in off-duty personnel because they were going to put our reserve engine into service. I was assigned to that engine, and we stood guard at the mansion along with the Rescue and some police department officers from late afternoon until 8 a.m. the next morning. There were some rumors about someone possibly flying a small plane into the mansion. This was the first time I had ever heard of a plane possibly being used as a terrorist weapon. I did not know it at the time, but things were about to change.

Supper was sent up to us, and we all experienced a quiet night. I never did see the Shah. If he were in the mansion I'm sure he was told to stay out of sight. As daybreak came we were ordered to return to headquarters. After a couple of cups of coffee and some conversation with the oncoming shift about our experience, I headed home ending a very strange and different shift.

The policy between the police and fire departments was changed after that incident so that either department would inform the other of what was going on in the city so there were no surprises.

High-Rise Fire Emergency

I was working at headquarters, assigned to ride on Engine 1, when about 20 of us were about ready to sit down for lunch that was interrupted by a general alarm for a high-rise fire on the southwest side of town. We headed south to Wilshire Blvd., turned west on Wilshire and headed for the Crocker bank building on the south side of Wilshire about ten blocks away. We pulled up front with nothing showing, so we went down the street on the west side of the building about a half block and parked.

A security guard met us at this point. We got our gear and he showed us what he thought was the best way in to the fire on the third floor. He took us through the parking area to a stairwell on the southeast corner of the building. This way in would later almost prove fatal.

We climbed the stairs to the third floor, put our air masks on and opened the door to the third floor hallway where we encountered medium smoke which became heavier the farther down the hallway we went. At about 100 feet the hallway turned 90° to the left. We began to feel the doors for heat and visibility was about zero. We ran into a wall and the hallway took another 90° turn to the left. About halfway down the hallway on the right we felt a door that was very hot.

We got our hose lines ready, which took a slight bit longer because of the heavy smoke, and we took a sledgehammer to the doorknob which took two or three swings because even with a flashlight it was hard to see. We finally freed the door from its lock and opened the door. Heavy fire met us, and we attacked it with 2 1/2-inch hose lines. We slowly worked our way into a large office, and after a few minutes we were making pretty good progress when all hell broke loose.

A large fire stream came in through the windows from the ladder pipe on the truck and blew off Bob Jeffries' facemask and knocked him down. His backup was Carlos Oseguera who helped Bob get to his feet and put his air mask back on. I was told this later, because I just heard this action through the smoke and fire. Then I heard a cry for help from someone in the hallway who said they could not breathe. I told Jim Anderson, my backup, to take the nozzle because I was going to see who was in trouble. I went out into the hallway and found two firemen with their five-minute low-air warning bells ringing. At first I didn't know who they were, then I recognized the muffled voices through the masks of Carl Urman and Larry Dowdle. Carl said he was out of air. Larry still had some. I found out later what happened to them. They got somehow disoriented and couldn't find their way out in the heavy smoke. I told them I knew the way out, but it was down this hallway which was U-shaped.

I grabbed Carl by the arm and Larry grabbed his other arm, and we ran down the hallway not being able to see anything. We ran until we hit a wall, then turned right and continued to run down this hallway when I heard the bell on my air tank go off. Carl was screaming he couldn't breathe. When we hit the other wall, we turned right and started to run. I thought to myself, *I hope Carl doesn't go unconscious on us, because if we have to carry him we are all going to run out of air*. We kept on running with Carl screaming "I can't breathe." We hit the next wall and I started feeling for door knobs on the right side of the hallway. I found a door and opened it. It was a phone room for all phone connections for that floor. The room was about eight feet long and six feet wide and clear of smoke. We all piled in. Larry said he was out of air, so I took my air tank and mask off to give to Carl and him and said I was going out into the hallway to find the stairwell, which I proceeded to do. I went to my left and felt for door knobs and found another door, and I opened it. It was the stairwell clear of smoke.

I was having a difficult time breathing, so I took a deep breath of fresh air and went back to get Carl and Larry. When I opened the door, the phone room was now half full of smoke. I told them, "I found the stairwell. Let's get the hell out of here!"

Larry and I picked Carl up. He said my tank was empty, and I told him to leave it. We assisted him to the stairwell, and he was a very groggy man. Larry and I half carried him down the stairwell and through the garage to a waiting Rescue where they assisted his breathing and transported him and Larry to UCLA. The other paramedics assisted me with some air, and after a few minutes I was okay. They also had to transport Capt. Jim Baron who was having a heart problem. We finally extinguished the fire, picked up our equipment, and returned to the station for a very late lunch.

Larry Dowdle was released from the hospital, but Carl spent five days at UCLA in Intensive Care for a very bad case of smoke inhalation. When he was released and on his first shift back, we all responded to a call that turned out to be nothing, and while we were there he ran up to me and thanked me for saving his life. He said the doctor told him if he had been in that smoke environment one more minute, he would not have made it.

I told him, "That's our safety net in there looking out for each other, and with God's help we make it out. It was my turn to help you, and tomorrow it may be your turn to help me or someone else, and that's the way it goes."

On the fire department today they have improved the breathing apparatus somewhat in that they have a buddy breathing connection on the mask where two people can breathe off the same tank. If that equipment had been available to us back then, Carl would not have had to go to the hospital.

After the fire was out and the smoke had cleared, we found another stairwell 50 feet from the office fire. Had the security guard taken us to that stairwell, Carl would have never spent five days in the hospital.

Lyle Slater taking oxygen after performing a rescue of two firemen at the Crocker Bank building on Wilshire Boulevard

The Edmund Fitzgerald, November 10, 1975

The Sir William Fairbairn, the ship on which Lyle Slater served

I had just arrived at old headquarters to start my 24-hour shift, had changed into my uniform and was walking out to the dining room for a cup of coffee, when I passed this little cubbyhole area where each man has a mailbox. I noticed a letter in my mailbox, so I took the letter to the table, picked up a cup of coffee and opened the letter. It was from a neighbor and good friend of my parents who lived in Ohio.

Her son was a good friend of mine in our early teen years before he passed away from a miss-diagnosed spleen infection, which devastated her and her husband. He was their only child. Her name was Mrs. Lewis and her late husband, Dave, was a sea captain who sailed iron ore ships all over the Great Lakes.

When I graduated from high school in the summer of 1954, I was working with my dad at the Berea bus lines. My dad was a mechanic and a body and fender repair man. He fixed all the wrecks and painted the buses when they needed painting. It was about the end of June while I was helping my dad paint a bus and trying to decide what I was going to do with my life, when I received a phone call from Mr. Lewis who asked me if I wanted to go sailing with him that summer and fall.

I talked it over with my dad, and he told me to go for it, that it would be a good experience, which it was. I got my merchant seamen license and a week later when Mr. Lewis sailed into Cleveland, Ohio, with a load of iron ore for the U.S. steel mills, I joined him and sailed for two seasons. A season would start in April and go through December when the lakes would freeze over. I sailed on the Sir William Fairbairn, a small ship as ore boats go, about 500 feet long. She was an old ship, about 58 years old, and because she was small she could get into a lot of different ports that the larger ships could not get into. So this was good for me, because I had a chance to see a lot of different things, and we carried a lot of different cargo, like iron ore, coal, salt, and flax seed. It was a great experience that helped me prepare for the fire department, which I had not yet considered.

I worked from 8 a.m. to 5 p.m. as an assistant to the three engineers who took care of the engine room. I would help them repair any pump or engine part. I learned a lot in this role, and I learned how to get along with people in close quarters with all different types of personalities and ages, and that would come in handy when I became a fireman ten years, later. It was exciting! We ate very well, and we went through a lot of big storms and drank a lot of beer when we hit port.

The reason Mrs. Lewis sent me the letter was she thought I might be interested in knowing that her husband, who had passed away a few years, ago, had a best friend who was First Mate on the Edmund Fitzgerald when it went down. She said, "I thought you might like to know, because you sailed with Dave, and you were his friend back then."

I thought a lot of her and her husband. They went through hell when they lost their only child, David, at 13 years of age. About two months later, my wife and I flew to Ohio to visit my parents' relatives and our friends, and when we visited my wife's sister, she told me that David, her oldest son, had a good friend from Sunday school who was a deck hand on the Edmund Fitzgerald when it went down. That was strange that I knew two people who had good friends who went down with that mighty ship and crew of 29 members.

Gordon Lightfoot wrote a song about the wreckage of the Fitzgerald, and if you ever hear that song, the twangy sound you hear throughout the song captures perfectly the sound of an 80-mph wind blowing through the superstructure of the ship. I know because I was in four or five bad storms where we saw 35-foot waves that would almost go over the pilothouse. That is where the wheelman steers the ship and the captain and first mate work.

One storm almost cost me my life, and I learned a valuable lesson. We were northbound, empty. We were going to Duluth and Superior, Wisconsin, to pick up a load of iron ore bound for the steel mills in Cleveland, Ohio. We were going out to White Fish Bay, the bay the Fitzgerald was trying to reach but never made.

I was visiting a friend, Bob Baehr. I went to school with him, and he also was a friend of the Lewis family. Bob was a deckhand on the Fairburn and had just finished helping the deck crew move the Fairbairn through the Soo locks. I visited with him for a while when I noticed the ship was starting to roll and pitch. I thought I had better get back to my cabin in the stern of the ship. If we were going into a storm, I had to wear a safety belt that hooked onto a cable that ran down the center of the ship over all the cargo hold covers which stuck up about 12 to 14 inches. The cable covered about a 400-foot distance. So I hooked onto the cable and started my long journey to the stern. It was getting dark and some of the waves were making it over the side and were crashing over the cargo hold covers. That situation, according to one theory, is what took the Fitzgerald down. The cargo hold cover clamps were old and worn and were not weather tight, so every wave that crashed over the covers dumped water into the hold, unknown to the crew. After about ten hours or so, the mighty Fitzgerald was slowly sinking, and it went down with all 29 crewmen.

I made my way back to the stern. I was wet from the spray of the waves, and I could hear that tattle-tale sound of the wind blowing through the superstructure of the ship. I unhooked and had 40 or 50 feet to go around the rear cabins to get to the first interior door. I tried to time the waves, but just before I got to the door an unexpected wave about six-feet high hit me and threw me into the cabin wall. Then, the backwash started to pull me off the ship. I was lucky. I grabbed onto the one-inch cable that was a guard rail that ran around the ship. I grabbed with both hands and feet and was able to withstand the force of the backwash. I made it to the door seconds later and went down to my bunk, changed my clothes and wrapped up in two blankets to get warm. That ice-cold black kiss of death wave almost got me, and if it had, no one would have known I was missing until 8 a.m. when I would not have shown up for work.

I never went on deck again in a storm. The newer ships have catwalks over the cargo holds so crew members can walk from stem to stern without going outside. Some crew members go out there if the ship is empty and riding high in the water in a storm. They pump water into ballast tanks that run along the inside of the ship to bring it down into the water so it would not be so vulnerable to the waves, allowing the ship to ride much better in a heavy sea. The crew members had to check the water levels in the tanks with long rods. They had to be tethered at all times, and that has to be an E-ticket job.

That was the only close call I had. I think someone was watching over me that night. It was quite an adventure for an 18-year-old, sailing for two seasons. Every time I think about almost going over the side, I get the chills. The Edmund Fitzgerald 20 years later would sink 20 miles from the spot where I had that close call in White fish Bay.

The Boot

I was at old headquarters station this one evening when at about 10:00 p.m. we were instructed to respond up in Station 2 district to a structure fire. I was tillering Truck 4. We suited up and made our way north. On arrival we found a large single-story home with fire coming out three windows in the front.

Engine 2 was first on the scene and attacked the fire with a 1 1/2-inch line through the front door. Engine 5 took a line to the rear. Truck 4 was ordered to the roof to ventilate. After we knocked down the fire, we came off the roof and assisted in the overhaul operation. During this time in the smoke I somehow stepped on a red-hot coil spring from a large couch. The coil seared through the bottom of my Wellington boot, my foot, and then came out the top of my right boot.

It felt like a bee sting but about ten fold. Neal Renfro, another fireman, was just behind me, and I asked him to pull that damn thing out of my foot. He chuckled and asked, "How the hell did you do this, Slater?"

I said, "I don't know. It wasn't easy."

He then pulled it out, destroying his gloves in the process.

They sent me to the hospital for treatment of a puncture wound and burn to my right foot, and then sent me home for a few shifts. Because of that incident, the chief did some research on protective footwear for firemen and decided to outfit everyone with new boots by Chippewa. They had steel toes and steel inserts to protect the feet.

 Two weeks after I returned to work, a shoe salesman from the Chippewa boot company came out to our department and fitted us for new boots. A couple of weeks later, a pair of boots arrived for all fire personnel. The new boots did a good job of protecting our feet. They were a little heavy, but we got used to them, and firefighters still wear that type of boot today. Most changes in the fire service come from bad experiences, and this was a bad experience for me with a good result for our firefighters.

Lucille Ball

One evening I was working at the station located in the north end of town up in Beverly Hills. We were watching the Dodgers game when we received a call about a strong smell of smoke. So Captain Stan Speth, Engineer Renny Hicklin, Fireman Steve Hoffman and I responded to the address given, and a couple of minutes later we pulled up in front of this older but beautiful home. Stan, Steve and I went to the front door and when the door opened we were met by Lucille ball, which was a pleasant surprise. She invited us in and informed us that there was a strong electrical smell. As I walked in I could tell it was a transformer from a doorbell or a florescent light that had gone bad.

She showed us the room where the odor was strongest, and we found a florescent light fixture that was the culprit. We disconnected the light fixture and told her she would have to get an electrician to replace it.

Then she wanted us to check her alarm system to see if it was working properly. So we checked it, and it was okay. She was very appreciative and thanked us. As we walked out to the rig, I was thinking I always enjoyed her shows, but she was so different in person, not the scatterbrained hyper blonde with a squeaky voice. She was a very pleasant lady. I guess that's what they call "acting."

LA Gay Fire

It was mid afternoon and Engineer Gary Poitner and I were working an extra shift for overtime at Station 2 when we received a structure fire call in our secondary district. This is an area of Los Angeles that we can respond to faster than LA can, so we help them out that way and in return if we have a huge fire in our town that requires more personnel than we have on duty they help us. This is called mutual aid.

Capt. Ed Davis, Gary Poitner, Fireman Dennis Andrews, and I responded up north to a house fire. On arrival we realized the house was pretty well involved in fire. A neighbor was out front at the street and informed us that two gay men live there, and he thought they had gotten into a fight. One man had poured gasoline in the house and set it on fire, run out, then had second thoughts and had gone back in to rescue his partner and had not returned.

The fire was coming out the front door and also coming out two large windows to the right which was probably the living room. We could hear LA coming in the distance. The captain decided to not make a hydrant but to go straight in for a fast attack. LA would be there soon to back us up and take over. I grabbed the nozzle and Dennis backed me up along with the captain. We gave it a quick shot through both windows to knock the fire down a little and then started to attack the fire through the front door. We were making some progress when LA arrived on scene with a good water supply and attacked the fire through the windows and then came in behind us.

It wasn't too much longer and we had a pretty good handle on it. This was about the time our 500-gallon tank on the engine ran out of water. We backed out, and LA finished the job. We helped LA overhaul while looking for two bodies. The fire had been so intense because of the fuel used that some of the drywall had fallen on top of the bodies, and we had been walking over them before we realized this. When we uncovered the bodies, LA turned it into a crime scene. Overhaul was stopped except for extinguishing small fires until the proper investigating units arrived.

We packed up our equipment, returned to the station and replaced our hose with clean hose and cleaned our equipment to get back in service. I took a shower, got dressed and entered the kitchen to resume preparation that had been interrupted. It had been a tough day with two dead bodies.

One of the ways firemen handle a tough day is by sitting down together for a good meal. It's a family thing. I was the designated cook for the day, so I started supper. I cooked chicken fried steak, mashed potatoes with gravy, corn and prepared a salad. For dessert I made my mom's recipe for strawberry shortcake. She had a special cake recipe, and it was known throughout our department as mom Slater's Strongsvilleon Shortcake, a favorite dessert. Strongsville, Ohio, was where my parents lived and I grew up. A serving of shortcake was a six-inch piece of cake cut in half which filled the entire plate. Smashed strawberries were laid on the cake along with a slab of vanilla ice cream topped with more berries and a large spoon of homemade whipped cream. Only one guy on the department could eat more than one helping,

Engineer Dick Lapointe. He was a fairly small guy, but he could eat at least twice as much as anyone, and all firemen are big eaters. We were lucky after that meal that it was a quiet night.

When fire crews worked Christmas or Thanksgiving, they would invite their families to dinner. Lyle Slater poses here with his shift of personnel referenced in many of the stories in this book. (front row, left to right) Mike Downing, Chris Giatras, Captain Stan Speth, Tom Cass, Dale Nordberg, Lyle Slater, (back row, left to right) Chief Jeremiah Hayes, Kerry Gardner, Captain Casey Griffin, Joe LaFirenza, Robert Jeffries, Marcus Pierce, and Captain Art Davis.

The Yellow Cab Driver

I was working at the new Station 3 one morning when we received a full arrest call on Olympic Boulevard. As we pulled up in front of the house address we saw a yellow cab parked out front. About then Rescue 1 pulled up behind us. We gathered up our equipment and went inside and found a woman in her 60's lying on the floor unconscious.

The cab driver said he had arrived to pick her up, and before they could get out the front door she collapsed. He was the one who called us. We checked for a pulse and hooked her up to our equipment. She was straight line so we immediately went to CPR mode. I started chest compressions. Fireman Kerry Gardner started ventilation. Mark Pierce, better known as "Foggy," was on the radio talking to the doctor at UCLA. The other paramedic, Terry Chavis, started the IV. At one point the doctor ordered an epinephrine shot. This needle is huge.

The cabbie was sitting on the couch across from us taking this all in, and I'm sure he had never seen this before. Terry took this large needle and shoved it into her chest and into her heart and then injected the medicine and pulled the needle out, then with his fist hit the woman square in the chest with a "cardiac thump."

I looked over at the cab driver whose eyes were big as saucers, and I could tell by the look on his face that he probably thought if she had not been dead before, she surely was now. We worked on her for another ten minutes, were beginning to get a pulse, and it looked pretty good. She tried to take some breaths on her own. At that time the doctor told us to load her up, assist breathing, and get her in ASAP.

Before we left, Terry Chavis thanked the cab driver for calling and told him he had saved her life because we had arrived in time. Then he told him that he was sorry he had lost his fare, but that we had to take her to UCLA. The cabbie said, "Man, I never seen anything like this before."

I am sure that cab driver never forgot that cab call, and I'll bet he told the story many times. The woman did well and left the hospital a week or so later. That was one of 15 cardiac saves that I was privileged to be a part of in my 30-year career, and I painted another notch on my helmet.

Strange and Sad Things

The Beverly Hills Fire Department has been very fortunate in that it has never lost a fireman on duty from its inception in around 1928 until the time of this writing in 2012. There have been many close calls, and in some cases if things had gone wrong we could have lost most of a shift. Some say it's luck. I think in most cases a Supreme Power looked out for us. Over the years I worked on the department from 1964 to 1994 we experienced injuries like most departments; however, in the time I worked there a lot of strange and sad things happened to Beverly Hills firemen off the job, and in some cases to their family members.

I worked with Captain Al Sanchez, and my wife and I managed a 24-unit apartment building owned partly by him. One day after a heavy rain storm he left his home to take his dog for a walk. The dog returned home, but Capt. Sanchez was never seen or heard from, again. The story was that there may have been foul play involved, or he may have slipped or fallen into the LA River which was above normal levels from abnormally heavy rainfall. He had been known to walk his dog in this area. That was some 30 years ago.

Bob Neal, a fireman I worked with, was a commercial fisherman on his days off. It was a small, one-man boat operation. He left home one day with his dog, and when he did not return that afternoon as he normally would, the Coast Guard and friends went looking for him. After a while they found his boat going around in a circle with his dog on board, but Bob was not on the boat. The story was that the searchers think he may have gotten hooked in the netting as it went overboard, or he slipped and fell overboard. I was told he could not swim. As far as I know his body was never found.

I worked with Bob Davis, Andy Voloski, and Don Sission. These three guys came down with Reiter's Syndrome, almost at the same time. This is a very rare disease with only a very few cases a year in the United States. It is a rare type of arthritis that makes all joints hurt. These three men had to retire, because they could not do the physical job that a fireman must do. They never found out why they came down with this disease, but they may have been exposed to something on the job.

When I had been on the department around a year, I was asked if I wanted to go on an deer hunting trip in Idaho with Don Grish, Bob Marshall, Kenny Linch, and a pilot who was a good friend to a bunch of guys in the department. I told Don I had given up hunting years ago when I was pheasant hunting back in Ohio. I shot a rabbit one day, and when I picked it up, it was not dead, and it was screaming because of the pain. I had to put him out of his misery, and I said, "I don't need to do this anymore." So when I arrived home I placed my shotgun in the closet and never shot it again, although it stands in the ready just in case someone comes into my house to do me or my wife bodily harm. I would not hesitate to shoot it again in self defense. I thanked Don for the invitation to hunt, but I was not interested, so they asked another fireman, Rob Roy Haler, to take my place. A few days later they left for Idaho for a three or four-day hunting trip. On the flight back home they ran into bad weather and the plane, investigators concluded, was overloaded with deer meat. The plane went down and they all lost their lives. That was a very sad time on our department. We attended five funerals over a very short period. I can't imagine what the New York Fire Department went through after 9/11 with 343 fatalities.

Bob Davis was a good friend of mine who I worked with for a few years before he had to retire because of an illness. His mother, who I knew very well, was a stand-in for Janet Leigh, the movie star. She lived in a nice neighborhood just south of Beverly Hills. One day she was murdered in her home. Bob Davis and his wife, Linda, called me from Idaho where they had moved and informed me of what had happened. They never found the killer for 25 or 30 years until they started to use DNA. They found this person, who was 21 years old at the time, who had lived for a while next door to Bob's mother. His modus operandi was the same as other victims in the area. They convicted him of the murder and sentenced him to life in prison.

I worked with Tom Crewse who one day at headquarters over a cup of coffee told me this sad story. His father and younger sister a few years ago were going on a trip, and they were on standby. Tom's mother worked for the airline and was able to get free tickets often on standby. They took the place of two no-shows. The plane left LA and was flying over the Grand Canyon area, when the TWA and a United airliner collided and crashed into the Grand Canyon killing everyone. A few years later before Tom became a Beverly Hills fireman he worked as a real estate agent. He received a call from a man who wanted him to list his house, so Tom went to this guy's house. Tom met him and wife, and Tom said the guy was obnoxious. During the conversation Tom asked why he was selling his home. Somehow, traffic was mentioned. Tom asked if the clients were selling because of the volume of traffic, and the man said, "No, I love traffic." Tom thought that was a strange response, because no one in California likes traffic jams. So this guy proceeds to tell him that he and his wife were going on a trip and got stuck in heavy traffic that made them too late for their flight. The plane left without them and was involved in a mid-air crash over the Grand Canyon. Tom said he could feel his blood start to boil, and he knew he had to get out of there, fast. Without a word he picked up his briefcase and left them sitting there wondering what had happened.

I worked with Rod Belanger for years, and I remember him telling me stories about his days. He was a submariner on the U.S.S. Amberjack during the Korean conflict. After he retired he and his wife, Candace, moved to Palm Springs. They had a son, Brian, who was a crewman on a tugboat in Southern California. On one night Brian was at work on the tugboat that was pulling a large barge full of rock from Catalina to San Pedro. The rock was for a breakwater project. As they were making their way to San Pedro some 25 miles from Catalina, a nuclear U.S. submarine was sailing to San Diego Naval Base to be used in the movie, *The Hunt for Red October*. The submarine passed submerged between the barge and tugboat which were separated by 600 feet. The tow line between the two vessels was about 20 feet underwater, and the sub's conning tower hooked onto the tow cable, pulling the tug under with three crewmen aboard. Two of the crewmen barely survived, but Brian did not. He was last seen trying to check out the engine compartment.

Another strange part of this story was that my son and his Boy Scout troop along with me spent a weekend at the naval base. We stayed in the dorms and ate in the mess hall with the sailors. One of the side trips we attended was a tour of the submarine used in the movie, *The Hunt for Red October*. At that time I had no knowledge of this submarine being involved in that sad, deadly accident that killed my friend's son, Brian. We found out later.

When I joined the department in 1964 I was told a story a couple of different times by different old-time fire personnel. It was about a young Howard Hughes flying a small plane over Beverly Hills. He had to make an emergency landing in town near a golf course, and an off-duty fireman was near the scene and was able to get Howard Hughes out of the plane's wreckage before any rescue personnel arrived. Howard Hughes was so thankful for the fireman's help, that he made his effort worthwhile. The men who told me this story have been long gone, but they did work with this fireman at the time.

Jack Secord was an engineer for the Beverly Hills Fire Department and a good friend. One Thanksgiving while we worked together he was having a big Thanksgiving dinner for his whole family. As his mom and dad were driving to his house, they were killed in an auto accident. The Jack I knew was never quite the same after that.

Chuck Oseguera, a good friend and Beverly Hills fireman, in 1978 was on a strike team fighting a fire in Mandeville Canyon just east of Malibu. Another fire started in the Agoura area northeast of Malibu. Chuck and his wife, Louise, lived in Agoura, and the fire came through their area driven by high winds. Their house burned to the ground. Both fires burned all the way to the beach in Malibu, and that is where I lived. My house was spared, and that is another story.

Protecting the President

At our shift meeting at headquarters one morning Captain Jerry Taillon told us that President Reagan was coming to Beverly Hills for an event. He would be flying in by helicopter from LAX and would be landing on the Beverly Hills High School football field.

This appearance would be a big event with many departments involved. Beverly Hills Fire Department would provide two engine companies with four men on each rig and one rescue with two paramedics. Capt. Taillon explained what to expect and what we had to do with the equipment. This would all happen on our next shift.

The morning of our next shift I was on Engine 1 along with Fireman Joe LaFirenza, Captain Speth, and Engineer Gary Poitner. About 9 a.m. we made our way down to the football field along with Rescue 1 and a reserve engine with Capt. Ron May in command.

On arrival we laid a 2 1/2-inch line from a hydrant nearby onto the near end of the football field, then connected the 2 1/2-inch line to the engine and laid out two 100-foot-long 1 1/2-inch hand lines. Capt. Ron May on the reserve rig did something similar. Rescue 1 positioned themselves for easy access to the landing pad area. This was all done in case there was a mishap on landing. This was standard procedure.

I was amazed at how many people were involved performing various tasks, probably 200 people including the FBI, Secret Service, LAPD, Beverly Hills PD, Sheriff's Department, and so on. The Beverly Hills football field was near a number of high-rise buildings on its west side in Century City. I was told that most of these buildings had sharpshooters on their roofs and also on some smaller buildings in our town.

We were in our fire gear and were eagerly waiting for the President's arrival. After about a half hour we could hear the choppers coming in the distance. When they arrived a couple minutes later we saw two of the most beautiful olive-drab helicopters I had ever seen. They were polished to the hilt. They landed one at a time about 100 feet or so in front of us. I was told they travel in twos, and you never know for security reasons which one carries the President.

The minute they were on the ground and cut the engines a black limousine pulled up to a chopper in front of us. The door opened, the stairway unfolded, and President Reagan waived and saluted us as he made his way down the stairs as fast as possible and was escorted to the waiting limousine by the Secret Service. They drove off as quickly as possible being escorted to the hotel where he would be staying by a number of police officers on motorcycles in front of the limousines and also in the rear.

We were impressed with how everything was so well coordinated. After everyone left except the two helicopters and the pilots, we were able to talk with the pilots and walk around the aircraft. One of the pilots gave Capt. Ron May a handful of matches with the Presidential Seal on them. He passed them out to all of us for souvenirs, then the two pilots boarded their helicopters and took off for LAX. We picked up our equipment and returned to the station with another different but great experience under our belt.

Man from Auschwitz

We responded to a heart attack call in the Threes district on the south end of town. We arrived on Engine 3 in front of a five-story apartment building, and Rescue 1 pulled up behind us. We unloaded and took the stretcher along with all of our other equipment and took the elevator to the fifth floor. When we entered the apartment we found an elderly gentleman complaining of severe chest pain. He was there with his wife and his sister, and they were very anxious.

The paramedics got his history, hooked him up to the equipment, started an IV, and contacted the doctor in the emergency room of the hospital. As I was setting up the IV bag I noticed numbers tattooed on the patient's arm. His wife saw that we had noticed them and told us he was an Auschwitz concentration camp survivor when he was a boy during the war.

Paramedics Mike Smollen and Casey Griffin were informed by the doctor to administer nitro and load him up and transport him pronto. When we were about to leave, the patient asked his wife and sister for a kiss. They were going to follow us in their car to the hospital. They kissed him, and we left the apartment and entered the elevator where the patient went into full arrest. We entered CPR mode. He must have known he was going out and that's why he wanted to kiss his wife and sister.

I drove the rescue and Casey, Mike, and Alan Coffield worked on the patient in the back compartment of the rescue all the way to Cedar Sinai Hospital. They did all the magical stuff that normally works on a full arrest, but nothing seemed to help. When we arrived at Cedars Sinai 15 minutes later, one doctor and two nurses were waiting for us outside the emergency room door. We unloaded the patient, continued CPR, and wheeled him into the emergency room. There we transferred the patient from our stretcher to their table and hospital personnel took over.

We collected replacement equipment, changed the sheets and pillowcases on a stretcher and sanitized the stretcher and equipment. A nurse advised us that the doctor after a 15-minute effort to revive the patient had pronounced the Auschwitz survivor dead.

It seems strange to me how we can respond to a full arrest, the patient can be down for five minutes, unconscious, and we can bring the patient back and he survives the heart attack. And then we go on a call like this one where the patient is alert and talking to you, then goes out and nothing you do can revive him. The only way I can look at it is we are God's instruments to keep the patient safe, as comfortable as possible, and give him or her our best shot. Then God decides when to call his people home.

Large Garage Fire and Explosion

One late morning while I was on Engine 5 at old headquarters we responded to a garage fire in the Engine 3 district. On arrival we found a five-car garage located in the rear alley behind these apartment buildings completely engulfed in flames. Captain Ron Savolskis told Bob Davis and me to take a 1 1/2-inch line down the alley, and as we were pulling the line toward the fire, I could see Bob Jeffries pulling a line off Engine 3 that was parked at the other end of the alley. We all arrived at the fire at about the same time.

I signaled Engineer Harold Dean to turn the water in from Engine 5. Bob Jeffries and another fireman started their attack on the fire from their side of the garage, and I was on the nozzle with Bob Davis backing me up on the other side. As we started our attack about 20 feet separated our line from Jeffries' hose line.

We had begun to get control of the fire when an explosion launched a large ball of fire out of the middle of the garage at Jefferies and me. Because we were fighting an outside fire we did not have our air tanks and masks on, so when the ball of fire hit us in the face it singed our eyebrows and burned our faces making us look like we had bad sunburns. The heat singed Bob's lungs but not mine. We figured Bob was either closer or he was inhaling while I was exhaling.

Regardless, this event caused him some breathing and lung problems for a while after the fire.

We finally extinguished the fire and thought the explosion was from a car's gas tank. Further investigation by us and the fire marshal revealed four or five gas cans stored in front of a car. This was a time in California when we were going through the first gas crunch where everyone owning a vehicle was standing in long lines for a limited amount of gas at every gas station in the LA area.

So someone was storing gas in the garage, and we had no idea. It goes to show that on this job you never know what you are walking into. Had we been in closer we could have been seriously injured.

Was that luck or something else?

The policy from then on was everyone involved in any type of fire fighting would wear full breathing apparatus whether it would be a car fire, garage fire, Dempsey dumpster fire or whatever.

Bob and I were treated for minor burns and returned to duty to finish our shift. From that day on every time we responded to a garage fire we had illegal gas storage on our minds.

Fireman or Firefighter

*W*hen I was hired on the Beverly Hills Fire Department in October 1964, on my first day with the department I was issued all my equipment including a beautiful, shiny silver badge with dark blue letters which read, "Fireman Beverly Hills Fire Department" and the number 15, my ID number. I wore that badge every 24-hour shift for some 20 years. One day the department issued everyone a new badge just like the other badge except it was silver and gold with blue letters reading "Firefighter Beverly Hills Fire Department."

The reason for the change was that women were getting interested in the fire service, and some of them were making their way onto some departments across California. This would make big changes in our department over the coming years.

When they tore down and rebuilt all of our three stations two of them still were not built with women in mind and had to be adapted later. The last new station to be built was a headquarter station designed to accommodate women so they would have their own bedrooms and restrooms. The firehouse language would be cleaned up, and so on.

When I retired in December 1994 there were no women on the department. Some did take the entrance exam but were eliminated along with many male applicants. In 2011 there were two young women on the department. Amy Horst, who came on the department in 2000, was promoted to the rank of Engineer. The engineer is a person who takes care of and drives the engine or truck to the fire scene and then operates that equipment while on scene. The second woman firefighter in 2011 was Melissa Hillis, hired in 2008. She also would study for the position of Engineer. I was recently told she was promoted to Engineer.

Gender prompted the distinction between "Fireman" and "Firefighter." When the badge switch was made the department gave firemen a chance to buy the old badges back for a keepsake, which everyone did. The badges were encased in a block of clear plastic with the fireman's name inserted at the bottom. The reason for this plastic was to ensure that if the badge were to fall into the wrong hands, the encased badge could not be used to impersonate a firefighter.

It makes a nice keepsake, and I have it displayed with my other badge which was mounted on a beautiful oak plank and presented to me at my retirement dinner held at the Beverly Wilshire Hotel in 1995. Also presented to me were my helmet and another beautiful plaque with a small axe mounted on wood given to me by the Beverly Hills Fire Association to recognize my 30 years of service. I have all of this displayed in my tavern, or as they call it in Kentucky, my "man cave," along with all the other fire memorabilia I have collected over the years.

Lyle Slater's new "Firefighter" badge

Gas Spill in a High-Rise Office Building

I was working at the new Station 3 at around noon as the four of us were preparing lunch when a call came in regarding an obnoxious odor in a high-rise building on the north side of Wilshire Boulevard. We responded and pulled up in front of this eight-story office building.

As we walked up to the building we encountered a strong smell of gasoline coming out the front entrance of the building. The engineer of the building met us in the lobby. Captain Wynn asked him what was going on and what was with the gas smell. The engineer informed the captain that he did not know, but he had a crew on the fifth floor doing some remodeling. The captain ordered the engineer to bring all elevators to the ground floor and shut them down, and we would meet him on the fifth floor using the stairwells.

We climbed to the fifth floor in full gear and found a crew pouring gasoline on the floor in the process of removing floor tiles and the glue which held them down. The foreman on the job approached us and the captain asked him what he was thinking using gas in a high-rise building. Before he could answer, captain said, "Stop everything you're doing. Shut off all power tools. We have to get this gas and fumes removed from the building as fast as possible."

The foreman started mouthing off to the captain, and I was expecting this place to explode at any moment. I told the foreman to shut up and do exactly what the captain said, because he had put everyone in the building in jeopardy. The captain radioed headquarters asking for a full response, that we had an eight-story building full of gas fumes which we had to get cleaned up and evacuate the building.

The captain asked the foreman how much gas was on the floor. He said about five gallons. I quickly calculated from what I had learned in an arson class that every gallon of gas was equivalent to 17 sticks of dynamite. We had a very hairy situation. We had to eliminate everything that might cause a spark. The other companies arrived on scene and started to evacuate the building using the stairwells.

Gas is heavier than air, and that's how the gas fumes made their way down the elevator shaft to the front entrance. Any spark where the mixture was just right would have put the building in orbit.

When it was over I was glad to exit the building and get some fresh air. Everything went well.

We could say we were lucky, but I think we had somebody watching over everyone in that building that day.

I had heard they took the foreman off to jail for endangering people's lives. We picked up our equipment and returned to the station for a very late lunch.

Waterous Pumps

I was working at old headquarters one morning, and I happened to be on the apparatus floor when a middle-aged man walked in the front door and approached me to ask if anyone would be interested in helping him sell some small portable fire pumps that had a small gas engine and could float on water.

I told him I lived in Malibu and would be interested, so he told me this story of how he had gotten to this point. He said he lived in the Hollywood Hills, and this fall they had a brushfire there which was threatening his neighborhood. Everyone in the neighborhood was on their roofs with garden hoses watering down their roofs, and they were using up so much water, which normally happens in a brushfire. He had very little pressure and almost no water. When he looked down into his swimming pool, which had 40,000 gallons, he thought to himself, *How dumb is this? I have all the water in the world down there, and I need that water up here.*

He said he was lucky that the fire department got the fire under control before it got to his house, but the fire did damage houses on the perimeter of his neighborhood. He said he will never be in that situation, again. So he started to do some research on pumps and came up with this "Waterous Pump" which the smoke jumpers use when fighting timber fires in

Washington, Oregon, Colorado, and other places. It was a gas-operated pump about the size of a medium-sized suitcase, and it had a floatation collar which completely surrounded the motor. It weighed about 60 pounds. The unit could be placed in any water source, including lakes, ponds, creeks, streams, or swimming pools, and could generate 50-foot stream of water through a 1 1/2-inch hose, nearly as good as a hose from a fire engine.

The next morning when I finished my shift I visited his office in Beverly Hills and saw the pump. I was impressed with the demonstration and told him I thought it was what residents in Malibu with swimming pools needed. So he gave me a pump for demonstrations, and on my days off I started selling pumps in Malibu. People were happy to have such a pump. They could use it in an emergency or leave it by the pool for the fire department to use.

I was so sold on the pump that I set up a demonstration at our headquarters station to show how the pump could be used to fill our engine tanks if there were no hydrant or if water pressure were too low. All that was needed was a swimming pool or any source of water, and you were in business. Everyone was so impressed, including the chief. We always sent two engines from our department on a strike team, and I thought it would be a good idea if each engine had its own pump. The chief liked the idea but was dragging his feet for some reason, until one day he sent our engines out on a brushfire call and they ended up on a ranch with no water except for a large pond. They lost some of the structures and almost burned up a $400,000 engine. The next day that I worked, the chief called me into his office to talk pumps. He bought two pumps, one for each engine that would go on a strike team from our department.

The pumps came in handy, including one time when we were sent to Mammoth Mountain, 150 miles away, where they dammed up a small creek and used the pumps to fill the engine. They had plenty of water. Occasionally, I would run into some of the Malibu residents who had bought the pumps for their pools, and they said it was the best investment, almost like having their own fire engine at their house.

Fourteen-Year-Old Girl Overdose

We responded early in the evening on Engine 1 from new headquarters to an overdose call with Rescue 1. We all arrived on scene at the same time, got our equipment and were met at the front door by the parents and sister who were all hysterical. The mother screamed, "Save my daughter!" The parents said she had taken something and they couldn't wake her.

Their 14-year-old daughter was in bed and unresponsive, so we checked for pulse and finding none immediately put her on the floor and started CPR. No one could tell us how long she had been down. I was doing chest compressions. We would get a pulse and then it would fade. We thought we might have a good chance with her because of her age.

We worked on her it seemed like an hour. She would fade in and out, then the doctors communicated over the radio to transport her to Cedar-Sinai Hospital which we did doing CPR all the way into the emergency room. A doctor and two nurses were waiting for us at the front door of the emergency entrance. We all assisted in getting her into the emergency room while continuing CPR.

Then they took over. We restored all of our equipment and the emergency room crew worked on her for another 20 minutes or so. Before we left the doctors pronounced her dead, and then they had to tell the family the sad news. I am glad that was not my job. We all felt bad for the girl and her family. What a waste of a young life.

That was the longest time that I have ever done chest compressions. I felt like I had done 2000 push-ups. We gave her our best, but sometimes you lose the battle. In this case she had been down too long before our arrival.

When my daughter and son went through the turmoil of their early teens, I relayed this story to them, and I hoped and prayed that they would remember it if they were tempted to do something stupid. They made it through those teen years, but my experiences with the department and the normal anxieties of parenting put a few gray hairs on my head.

The Slater Sling

$\mathcal{E}$arly in my career I took a lot of fire suppression and tactics classes provided at night at Santa Monica Community College. One class I was taking addressed highrise fire tactics, and for part of the class the instructor showed a film of the New York fire Department and how they operate at a high-rise fire.

One of the problems we had in Beverly Hills in a highrise fire situation was carrying all the equipment to the upper floors using the stairwells. We never used an elevator because they have been known to take you to the fire floor, which is not good. Every firefighter carried his own breathing apparatus strapped on his back, but taking extra air tanks was a problem, because if you carry two extra air tanks, one in each hand, they tie your hands up and every time you have to open a door you have to set them down, open the door, and pick them up again.

Handling the air tanks is very time consuming when you're in a hurry. In the New York film firemen used some type of strap that was hooked to two air tanks and placed on their shoulders leaving their hands free. This approach looked like a great idea. After the class I asked the instructor who was a fire captain from LA if those straps were available for purchase. He said he didn't think so, but that straps were a good idea. On my next shift I collected a bunch of material we had around the department and made some prototypes until I had one that worked quite well. I used old 2 1/2-inch hose that had been condemned because of age and cut it into 14-inch sections that would be used as a shoulder pad so it would not cut into a fireman's shoulder. Then I took some new 1/2-inch nylon rope which we had plenty of for the straps which would hook onto two air bottle valves and air outlet. I then used some large washers and bolts to hold it together and installed a slip ring to secure the tanks from falling off the strap.

On my next shift I showed the setup to Chief Bill Daley. He liked what he saw and asked if I could make two for each fire rig on the department. On my next shift Chief Daley wrote me a letter and posted a copy on the bulletin board making it official that this equipment be placed on all fire rigs. It would be called the "Slater Sling," and I would teach a class on its use. They work very well and are in use today. They may use some different materials, but it's the same idea and works the same.

Arsonist

Many of the firemen I worked with took fire investigation and arson classes, which were very interesting subjects to study, and some of the guys took these arson classes from Capt. John Orr who worked for the Glendale Fire Department. He was a well-known and highly-respected arson investigator throughout the state of California.

A good friend and colleague of mine, Mike Smollen, had taken classes taught by John Orr and was impressed by him. When Mike went to work in our fire prevention bureau, he became our arson investigator and would call on John Orr for some advice in solving fire investigations in our city. They became friends.

Over a two-year period fire conventions were held in Northern California, and John Orr would be one of the speakers. John Orr would be called in to solve a rash of fires up and down the coast about the time of these conventions. He would be able to tell where the fires had been started and what type of delayed starting devices had been used.

A sharp captain who worked for the Bakersfield Fire Department put two and two together and came up with a theory that no one believed, but after about two years when John Orr's fingerprints were found on a delayed starting device that was not destroyed, John Orr was convicted and sent to prison for life. One of the fires had killed four people including a little boy. Mike Smollen and everyone who knew John Orr was stunned and shocked.

Every profession can have a bad seed among its employees, but when scandal hits fire or police departments, which are held to higher standards than other agencies, it's embarrassing, and it hits to your core when someone tarnishes your profession and the job you love and are willing to put your life on the line for.

I did take an arson class from a Los Angeles fire captain who I thought was pretty sharp. Mike Smollen later became a battalion chief and is now retired from the Beverly Hills Fire Department. Best-selling author Joseph Wambaugh wrote a true story about John Orr called *Fire Lover* that became a television documentary.

Stabbing at the Beverly Hills Hotel

*A*rescue call at 3:10 a.m. regarding a stabbing at the Beverly Hills Hotel came in over the intercom at the new Station 2. I had been in a deep sleep and was a little groggy as I jumped into my turnouts.

As we pulled up the circular driveway at the hotel, Rescue 2 was on our tail. We gathered up our equipment and went inside where the clerk at the front desk said that the security guard was on the second floor. The police arrived at that time, and we took the elevator to the second floor. We noticed blood on the floor of the elevator and on the elevator panel. We arrived at the second floor, the door opened, and we saw a trail of blood all the way to the room. The room looked like a slaughterhouse with blood splattered all over the floor and on most of the walls and ceiling.

The security guard was trying to stop the bleeding on a man lying on his back by trying to stuff a pillow around his neck. They were both covered in blood. The man's neck was cut from ear to ear. The story was a hotel guest picked up another man in the bar downstairs at closing time about 2:30 p.m., and they went up to the room where a fight broke out and the man from the bar broke a glass ashtray, cut the hotel guest's neck, then ran out and went down the elevator and disappeared.

This was a time when we first were hearing about a strange and deadly sickness called AIDS. There was not much information out on it, but we were told it was passed by homosexual activity and body fluids. We were in a room full of blood. We all scrambled for rubber gloves, but we could only find four pairs, and there were eight people in the room. Policy would change after this call. Two paramedics and the other firemen including me gloved up and did what we could to stabilize the patient. As I was assisting the paramedics, I looked around at the amount of blood this guy had lost and could not believe he was still alive.

My second thought was how we were in a profession where we would be awakened from sound sleep and confronted by this situation which seemed to be a bad dream. We somehow kept the man alive until we delivered him to the emergency room at UCLA where doctors were able to save the man's life. He did make a full recovery I was told later, and at that time they never found the other man.

Policy changed on our department from that day on where engine personnel coming on duty would check to see if there were at least one full box of rubber gloves on board the rigs. I will never again look at that beautiful Beverly Hills Hotel in quite the same way.

Rocket Man

I arrived at the new Station 2 to start my 24-hour shift, and as I walked into the kitchen to get a cup of coffee Tim Scranton, the other fireman sitting at the table, said, "Lyle, you will never guess who I spent the day with yesterday."

"Probably not. Who? Your hero, Buzz Aldrin? Sure, tell me another BS story."

"No, I am not kidding. Chief Daley and I took Buzz Aldrin all over Beverly Hills on the Fox," said Tim.

The Fox was a 1928 Ahrens Fox fire engine. When I came on the department in 1964 it was out of service and in the corner collecting dust. Someone in the upper echelon of the fire department or the city decided to send it to Chino Correctional Institution in Southern California for restoration.

When the inmates were finished, it was beautiful. Some of the old retirees said it looked better than when it was new. Tim was assigned to keeping it clean and shiny, and he also was assigned to be the designated driver for any special occasion, such as the visit by Buzz Aldrin. Tim proceeded to tell me that Chief Daley and he took Buzz Aldrin to every school in town where the astronaut gave a short talk and then passed out to students a pamphlet featuring the Declaration of Independence.

At some point Tim explained to Buzz Aldrin that he had a buddy (me) back at the station who was a space nut, and that he had read all the books written on the moon shot including Chuck Yeager's book. Tim asked Buzz to autograph one of the pamphlets for me.

Then Tim passed the pamphlet with autograph to me. I was so envious of Tim, but the pamphlet and signature eased that feeling. I thanked Tim and told him that the autograph was special. I told him, "Do you know you have the distinction of giving the slowest ride of 25 mph through Beverly Hills to Rocket Man, the fastest man on earth, who travelled at 25,000 mph going to the moon?"

Tim said, "I hadn't thought of it that way."

"That will be a good story to tell your grandkids," I said. He agreed.

I talked to Tim recently some 20 years after the fact to confirm the story and told him I have that Declaration of Independence pamphlet with Buzz Aldrin autograph framed and hanging in a special place in the Slater's White Horse Tavern along with all of my memorabilia of the fire department and also all my memorabilia of my 25 years of racing. The Tavern is a place I built on my 34-acre ranch, or "farm" as they call it in Kentucky, where my wife, Shirley, and I now live. The Tavern consists of a pool table, full bar, a card table, and a wide-screen TV to watch NASCAR and the UK basketball games.

In the wintertime I invite about 15 old friends in to play pool, eat pizza, drink beer, and tell tall tales. They are all good at doing all of that in Kentucky. They call a tavern like mine a "man cave."

Years later Tim Scranton became chief of the Beverly Hills Fire Department, and I am proud of him. I had a nickname for him when I was working with him. "Timothy O'Leary Scrantoneon." He is my good friend. We had a lot of fun working together years ago.

Beverly Hills 1928 Ahrens Fox Fire Engine

Angels in the Smoke

On my way home after working a 48-hour shift I stopped to help my wife, Shirley, set up her classroom for open house. She taught the gifted kids in the Santa Monica school district.

I was helping her for a couple of hours when the superintendent came into the classroom and asked us if we knew that there were two brush fires burning in Malibu where we lived. This was news to us, and we decided that I should check it out.

Driving down the coast highway toward Malibu I could see a large plume of smoke in the Topanga Canyon area located on the eastern edge of Malibu. On the radio they said a second brushfire was burning in the Decker Canyon area located on the northwesterly side of Malibu. Neither fire was in our area.

We have a good friend, Chris Cressey, living in the Decker Canyon area. She was a widow who had recently lost her husband to brain cancer. She lived in a very brushy area up the canyon, and I was concerned about her. I called Shirley and told her the story and that I was going to try and get to her home.

As I started up Decker Canyon, a very curvy canyon road, smoke got so bad I could hardly see the road in front of me, so I turned around. It would be very easy to run off the road and fall into this deep canyon.

I made my way back down the canyon road to the coast highway where I met a sheriff's car there with two deputies in it. They asked how the road was, and I told them I had driven up about a mile and visibility was so bad I had to turn around. They said they were going to give it a try. I told them I was an off-duty Beverly Hills fireman and asked if I could go with them. They were glad to have me go along.

As I climbed into the back seat, they told me to watch out for the wildcat. They had a bobcat in a cage on the back seat right next to me. I told them they would have to tell me that story some time, but we were so intent on making our way up the canyon road I never did get the story.

Smoke had lifted somewhat, and most of the time we could see a couple hundred feet in front of us. I told them I was trying to get to a friend's house, and they said let's give it a try. There was a stretch of road about 500-feet long just before her house where the trees on both sides cover the road. Just as we were about to enter that stretch of road, the trees burst into flames creating a tunnel of fire. The driver hit the brakes hard and said, "Let's get the hell out of here!" He reversed and floored it making that evasive turn you see on the cops shows on television. We drove through fire four or five times before reaching the coast highway. Lucky for us we had just enough visibility through the smoke to get there.

When I got out of the car I checked the doors on my side and the paint on the doors was blistered. I said, "Thanks for that E-ticket ride." They said it was spooky. I got in my car and headed back down the coast towards my house which was about 10 miles away.

I saw an engine company from LA stopped at a driveway. A car came down a long curvy driveway, and the driver asked the captain for some help. He had workers at his house to be evacuated, and his car was too small. I told the captain and him that I would take my car and help him, so we made our way up the quarter-mile driveway to his house. On our way up I could see the fire coming down into the canyon behind his house, and it would not be long before it would be on top of us.

The man told me to get his workers and he would get his housekeeper. I told his three workers to get in the car, and they said they were going to stay with the house and man the hoses that they were on. I said that's not a good idea, but I did not have time to argue. They looked determined to stay. The man got his housekeeper in his car and started down the driveway. The smoke now had arrived, and it was thick. I saw him drive off the driveway ahead of me into a smoke bank. I turned my lights on and blew my horn hoping he would see or hear me. I was able to make my way down the driveway a little farther until I could see no more. The smoke was so thick I had to stop. I could hear the roar of the fire coming. I thought I was going to burn up in the car. Just then for one second it was clear as a bell and then turned black, again, but in that instant in my mind I could see 100 feet of driveway, so I drove from memory and stopped. It was like when you turn a light on in a room that's dark and turn it off. You can see in your memory across the room. I waited for about a minute, and the same thing happened. It got clear as a bell then was socked in. I drove from memory, again. That happened two or three times before I was able to drive out of the smoke bank and could see the last 500 or 600 feet of driveway down to the coast highway. As I sped down the driveway, I looked in the mirror, and the guy and his maid were on my rear bumper. I was surprised, and the fire was on his rear bumper. The fire chased us down to the coast highway, and as we bounced across the road. He turned left and headed south to safety.

The LA fire crew was engaging the fire. I asked if they needed help, and the captain said they were okay. I headed north and was thinking to myself that must have been quite a show for the LA crew to see two cars come out of that smoke bank with the fire on our tails.

I also was thinking that someone was looking out for us to show us the way out. Thank you, God.

As I headed up the coast highway I was going to make another attempt to get to Cressey's house. I turned on to Decker Canyon, and the fire had blown through that area. I was able to make it all the way to her house. I was glad to see the house standing with everything else in ashes. She was happy to see me. I told her I had tried twice to get up there, and she said she was lucky that a Rolling Hills Engine was in the area, but it had no water. She had water stored in large trash cans, and that's how she saved the house. I said that must've been quite a firefight, and she said it was.

I checked her house for any signs of a rekindle, and everything looked okay. I asked her if she was going to be okay. She said she had been through the worst part and thought she would be okay. I gave her a big hug and left for home.

About two years later I was driving up the coast to Oxnard on my way to a dentist appointment. Tracy Van Blargen was a good friend and my dentist. We also raced go carts and midgets together for years. I passed that long driveway where we had that close call. I was wondering if that same man still lived there, and if he did, he might want to attend my son's class he was arranging for the Malibu community.

Marc, my son, was going for his Eagle Scout badge, and one of the requirements for that badge was doing some type of community service, so he chose to put on an emergency preparedness meeting.

My wife and I had been involved with the Malibu Emergency Preparedness Group for several years, and Marc thought that was a worthwhile organization. To prepare for the meeting he had to interview all emergency services, the fire department, sheriff's department, Red Cross, animal rescue department, and so on. He arranged for one person from each department to speak and give out pamphlets at his meeting. He also made signs to advertise the meeting, passed out materials at school, talked to the city council members and invited them to attend. He got permission to use the Malibu school auditorium to hold the meeting. He would be the master of ceremonies at the meeting, a big project for a 13-year-old.

On my way back from my dentist I drove up that driveway to the house, a much different experience this time. The house looked like it had survived okay. I knocked on the door and an elderly gentleman answered the door. I asked if he were the owner, and he said he was. I asked him if he had lived there during the fire two years ago, and he said yes. I asked him if he remembered a tan-colored Volkswagen that day, and he said, "Yes! Was that you? Oh, my God. I always wondered who you were." He then thanked me for saving their lives and noted, "When you honked the horn and turned on your lights, I followed your taillights. Every time you would move, I was right on your tail. I remember doing that quite a few times until we got out of that smoke. We got out of there just in time."

I told him someone was looking over us that day and showed us the way out.

He agreed and said, "I am glad you stopped." He said his house had suffered some damage, but that his workers had done a good job with repairs.

I told him the other reason I had stopped was that my son was going for his Eagle Scout badge and was preparing an emergency preparedness meeting for the community to get the badge. I said, "There will be a lot of information about brushfires and how to survive one. You survived one, but you might be interested in attending this meeting." He said he would.

My son had the meeting a week later, just before the brushfire season, and it was a big success with about 500 residents attending the meeting. A lot of good information was had by all. My wife and I were so proud of our son for doing such a good job at putting on that meeting. He became an Eagle Scout a few months later and was recognized by the city council for what he had done. My wife was so impressed with the speakers that night that she spent the next year researching, meeting with officials and writing the Malibu Emergency Preparedness Neighborhood Network Plan. The state published 500 copies to be distributed in Malibu.

It wasn't long before we experienced another fire in Malibu, and after it was over Marc received a lot of good compliments from residents who had attended that emergency preparedness meeting. People told him that the information they received that night had helped them through that fire. Some 22 years later Marc works for the Boy Scouts of America as a district manager up in the San Francisco area, and he loves his job.

The Best Little City Fire Department in the World, 1989

The duty captain called our morning meeting to inform us that the underwriters were coming to evaluate our fire department and city. They would be living with us for two weeks during which time they would be checking everything including our station's equipment, response times, water system maintenance, and general knowledge of every person on the job on all three shifts. We were advised that if we did not want to embarrass ourselves and make the department look bad we should start boning up on anything they might ask about the job.

This inspection was very important, because the rating would affect the insurance rates of the home and business owners. So we hit the books.

A week later five underwriters toured the station and called a meeting to explain their mission. They would be living at the station 24-7 for two weeks, responding to calls with us, and eating and sleeping at the station.

The guys on my shift did a pretty good job of preparing themselves. Most of our job is routine. When responding to calls we use basically the same equipment, but sometimes we might be called to use some equipment that we use once or twice a year. This is the equipment the captains would give classes on. I took my books out and went over some history of the city and the department that I was taught in my rookie class 25 years earlier.

The underwriters responded to calls with us, staying in the background on fire and medical calls to study our operation. They asked me five or six questions about my job as a fireman, and I had all the answers. They slept in the dormitories, they ate with us, and we swapped stories. All in all it was a pleasant experience. I think that was the general feeling throughout the department. One month after they left we received the report. The duty captain called us together and said we had done a good job because we received a Class I rating, the very best.

Only eight fire departments in the whole country had received a Class 1 rating, the highest fire protection service rating by the Insurance Services Office Commercial Risk Services, Inc. That made us proud. That rating meant homeowners would pay the lowest rates for insurance, and in Beverly Hills with the millions of dollars in property values, that was a good thing.

Shirley and I had a chance to travel throughout Europe two times, and some of our highlights were visiting fire departments in some of the larger cities. We enjoyed walking tours of Venice, Italy, conducted by an Italian fireman. We were invited to some homes for dinner and visited with their families, but all in all I didn't think I saw another fire department that was better equipped or trained than ours.

So if we were ranked eighth in our country, I think we were ranked eighth in the world, not bad for a small department with 85 men and three stations protecting one of the wealthiest towns in the world. I was proud to be a fireman for Beverly Hills, to work with the special men who came and went in the 30 years I was a fireman there.

Most Stressful Types of Emergency Calls

If you would ask firefighters across the country what types of emergency calls would be the most intense, stressful, and emotional, they would say a life or death situation involving infants and young children. Firefighters respond much faster to these types of calls, and when they arrive on the scene, they see their kids in them. If things don't go well, they live with it for a long time.

I remember responding to a SIDS death one evening at a time when the department had just finished rigorous EMT training taught by our paramedics. At about 10 p.m., Richard Perez and I were the firemen on Engine 3, and we responded with Rescue 1 on an unresponsive infant call. Our engine flew down there and arrived at the same time as Rescue 1 with paramedics Richard Rimp and Casey Griffin.

We all went to the front door, and it was locked. No answer. The captain told us to take the door out, so Richard Perez went to the rig for a sledgehammer. Casey and I decided not to wait, and we kicked the door in. We made a fast check. No one was home. By now Richard was returning with a sledgehammer, and he noticed a short distance down the street an elderly woman running toward him with an infant in her arms screaming, "Save my grandchild!"

Perez took the baby and immediately started CPR. By this time two Beverly Hills police cars screeched to a halt and officers ran toward Richard and the baby, then paramedic Rimp took the baby from Richard Perez and continued CPR. They quickly decided that paramedic Rimp would go with one of the police officers to UCLA hospital, because it would be faster in the police car. So they took off with Casey following in hot pursuit with the rescue unit.

We found out then that we had been given the wrong address, and the correct address was next door. The remaining officer was able to get the story from the grandmother who was babysitting the infant for the first time. This was the first time the young couple had ever left the baby, so this was a well-deserved night out for the young couple. The grandmother was so upset, and we all felt her pain. She said she had checked the baby earlier, and the baby was sleeping fine.

When the grandmother checked on the baby a little later she found the child unresponsive. She did nothing wrong, and yet I don't know how a person could ever get over something like this. It was the worst thing that could happen. The police officer tried to console her, and we repaired the door and left a note explaining what happened.

We returned to the station, and it was not long before Casey called with some very sad news that the baby had not survived. This was tough news for all of us. It was the first SIDS death that we all had experienced, and this affected me so much that when my two kids were born, I could not wait until they were past one year old when the chance of a SIDS death lessened.

Out at Home Plate

At 1 p.m. from new headquarters we were dispatched to Roxbury Park to respond to a full cardiac arrest. Along with Rescue 1 we arrived on scene and we could see people waving frantically near home plate on the baseball field.

Engineer Gary Poitner parked the engine some 300 feet away. The opening in the fence was not large enough for us to enter, but Rescue 1 was able to get through. Capt. Bill Daley and I along with the other fireman, Greg Vitali, ran to Rescue 1 that was just pulling up to home plate. Daley grabbed the defibrillator and Paramedic Bruce Mauer took the paramedic box. I went to the patient who had been the umpire for a Little League baseball game and had a heart attack. He was lying on home plate.

The patient had no pulse and was not breathing, so I started chest compressions. The other firemen started ventilating. Bruce and Capt. Daley, who was also a paramedic, started an IV. The other paramedic, Terry Sage, contacted the doctors by radio at UCLA. We were now in full arrest operation.

After a few minutes, we were starting to get a good response, and then at one point the doctors decided he should be transported immediately while we continued CPR. We loaded the umpire onto the stretcher and into Rescue 1, and the two paramedics along with Greg Vitali went in with the patient. I was told to drive.

Just as I started to leave, a little boy about ten years old ran up to me and said he was with the patient and asked to come with us, so I strapped him in the passenger side seat and headed for UCLA. The traffic was extremely heavy. I had to weave in and out of traffic going on the left and right side of Wilshire Boulevard all the way.

At one point I looked over at the kid. His eyes were as big as saucers. I am sure this was an E ticket ride for him. About halfway to UCLA we heard some chatter in the back compartment, and I heard the paramedic say the umpire was starting to come around. The kid heard this, turned around and hollered through the pathway between the cab and patient compartment, "Hold on, Dad!" Then I knew who this kid was, and I think I drove a little faster. As we pulled into UCLA Emergency, we were met by a team made up of one doctor and three nurses. They helped us wheel the patient into the ER, and then we lifted the patient from our stretcher to the ER table, and they took over. The kid stayed with us as we recouped our equipment so we could get back in service.

After a short time the doctor came out and told us the patient was doing fine. He had a good pulse and was breathing on his own. We told the doctor that the boy was the patient's son, so the doctor told him that his dad was doing fine and that the firemen had saved his life. With that the kid came around to each one of us and shook our hands and thanked us for saving his dad.

When he came to me and shook my hand, I was so happy for that little kid. I said I was glad I could help, and then I had to turn away because he brought tears to my eyes.

I could not believe how grown up and appreciative this kid was at ten years old.

That was what this job was all about and what made me want to get up in the morning, and I couldn't wait to get to work each day.

Two weeks later the umpire walked out of UCLA. I considered at that time it was a save, and I painted another Roman numeral on my helmet, which would be one of 15 numbers for lives saved from cardiac arrest by the end of my 30-year career.

As I was confirming the story years later I contacted Bruce and Bill before writing it. Bruce told me that the umpire had a young daughter there that day and the police officers took care of her. That was a surprise to me. Bruce also said that the patient came to the station numerous times to thank us for what we had done. I did not know that, either. I must have been off duty.

Ed McMahon

I was working at the new Station 2, and we were about ready to sit down for dinner. Tim Scranton, the other fireman, was cooking my favorite dinner, chicken fried steak. When the door bell rang, I answered it and Ed McMahon, Johnny Carson's sidekick, was standing there. His limousine had broken down out front, and he wanted to use our phone to see about getting another ride. This was before cell phones.

He made the call and was told it would be one hour before they could get another car. He told us he and his wife were going to the Beverly Hills Hotel which was located on Sunset Boulevard about two miles from our station. Capt. Pettinato suggested we could take him down there in the fire engine. Ed thought that would be great but wondered if there would be room for his wife.

We told him there was plenty of room, so we all piled into the engine. Rick Staral, Ed McMahon, and his wife got in the front seat, and Capt. Pettinato along with Fireman Tim Scranton and I got in the back seat and took off for the Beverly Hills Hotel. As we approached the driveway to the hotel the Capt. told Rick the engineer to turn on the red lights and siren, and we drove up this 500-foot driveway in impressive style and stopped at the front entrance.

All of Ed's friends were standing there, and when he opened the door and he and his wife stepped out, they about fell over and started laughing. One guy said, "Only you would make a grand entrance like this."

Ed thanked us, and we returned to the station and my favorite meal. Every year after that Ed McMahon and his wife would send us a case of fine wine for Christmas, which would be divided up at our Christmas party held at one of the big hotels in town.

Full Arrest on Wilshire Boulevard

I was on Engine 1, and it was late morning when we received a call for a man down on Wilshire Boulevard. We responded with Rescue 2, and as we pulled up a middle-aged man was lying on his back on the sidewalk with four or five people around him trying to make him comfortable.

He was conscious and complaining of chest pains, and he felt dizzy. We started an IV and were getting some information when he went unconscious and into a full arrest. We started CPR and the paramedics contacted UCLA Hospital. We were working on him about ten minutes when I heard a bus pull up behind us.

I heard a bunch of people talking a foreign language. I was doing chest compressions, and when I looked up about 50 Japanese men were surrounding us, and each one had a Nikon camera. Then we heard their cameras going off, chuck ching, chuck ching.

It turned out that they were a busload of Japanese doctors attending a convention, and they had never seen CPR performed. The procedure was new to us, and it had not yet been practiced in Japan. We had a good response with the patient and got him back into a good rhythm and breathing on his own before we left for UCLA.

So it was a picture-perfect rescue performed for all the Japanese doctors. I could tell they were impressed by their expressions and excitement. Our pictures were probably shown all over Japan as some of these doctors gave lectures.

I followed the patient's progress at UCLA, and when he was released I put another Roman numeral on my helmet going toward 15 lives saved in 30 years.

Straight into Hell

We were dispatched to a brush fire in Malibu one afternoon, and as we made our way up this curvy country road, we saw a Los Angeles fire rig parked off the road. They looked like they had been through hell and back. Their rig was filthy, and the men looked like they had been rolling around in an ash pile.

When one of the men saw us coming, he stepped out in front of us and hailed us down. As we pulled to a stop, this guy said, "My, God, don't get that thing dirty!"

I will have to admit I think our rigs were the best looking I had ever seen. The rig we were using was new, polished to the hilt with big aluminum rims so shiny you could see yourself in them, so we did look a little out of place, there.

Captain Pettinato opened the door and stood on the running board and said, "Hey, have you seen a Perrier water truck anywhere?"

The LA fireman said, "What?"

The Captain said, "Yes, we are from Beverly Hills, and we use nothing but Perrier water in this rig's water tank."

The guy started to laugh and said, "You got me, there." As we pulled out he said, "We left you a lot of fire."

The captain said, "That's what we're here for."

We drove up another mile and met a spotter who would take us to our first assignment, and as we followed him he took us straight into hell. I had never seen so much fire.

The spotter said, "Drop off here and help these engine companies the best way you can." It was a small subdivision, and most of the houses were on fire at various degrees, while others were about to be consumed.

We picked out one house we thought we had the best chance with and went to work on it. In a wind-driven fire like this one fire gets a good hold on a house, and it's almost impossible to save it. Usually, this type of fire is overwhelming, because you don't have enough manpower or water to cover everything. You give it your all, and sometimes you win and sometimes you lose the battle. With much effort we were able to save this house with minor damage, but there were some homes that were lost.

Later on in the middle of the night going to another assignment, we drove through this large bowl-like area that the fire had gone through a few hours earlier, and it was surreal, like being in a different world. This winding road went through the bottom of a bowl which was a mile or so wide in all directions. It was dark, and as far as you could see were red and yellow burning embers. It was like driving through the bottom of a large pot belly stove after the fire had gone out leaving yellow and red burning coals. It was very warm, maybe 115 degrees, and every once in a while the wind would gust and send sparks flying. I had never seen anything like it. I hate to say it, but it was beautiful.

Much later daylight broke, and I looked at George Richards, the other fireman, and started to laugh. I said, "George, do you remember those LA guys we saw, yesterday? Well, you look just as cruddy as they did." Then he started to laugh and told me to look in the mirror.

As the sun came up, we looked at Big Red, our fire engine, and it looked just like that filthy LA fire rig did. Yes, we had been through hell and back.

Later that morning things were getting under control, and we went to the command post for breakfast. After we ate, they cut us loose to return to our station. On the ride back I was thinking about the LA firemen. We had pumped a lot of water through our rig that night, and it wasn't Perrier. That LA fireman when he sees or hears "Perrier" will probably always remember that day.

Recently I talked to Dominic Pettinato about this story, and he remembered it the way I did. He lives up in Colorado Springs with his wife, Yvonne, and near his daughter and grandkids. Dominic said he told this story to a bunch of his friends, and they got quite a kick out of it, especially the Perrier part.

Don Rickels Fire in the Fireplace

I was working at Station 2, and we were half way through the spaghetti dinner I had cooked when we received a fire call for a fire in the fireplace. We all looked at each other, puzzled, wondering what's wrong with that.

We responded to an address just behind the station, and as we pulled up front of this large, single-story house, the front door opened and a gentleman stepped out. We could see black smoke pouring out over his head. As the gentleman got closer we could see it was Don Rickels. He looked funny. He had black soot all over his face, and he explained to us in his funny way what happened. He said his wife, God bless her, started a big fire in the fireplace and forgot to open the flu. She called for help, so he threw a pan full of water on the fire, and now there is smoke and debris all over the place. "Can you help me out?" he asked.

We unloaded and entered the house. The fireplace was huge. It looked like a fireplace for a lodge with a firebox so large that a person could almost walk into it. The fire was smoldering, and the flu was half open, so we opened it all the way. There was still a lot of smoke in the large room, so we set up smoke ejectors to clear the room. As we were doing this we were visiting with Mr. Rickels and his wife.

He was the nicest guy. I can see how he gets away with being so obnoxious, because his true personality is a nice and polite guy. So everyone who knows him understands that his on-stage behavior is a big act. I am glad I met him. I have a different opinion of him, now. We finished up, and Mr. Rickels and his wife were very appreciative of what we did, and they thanked us many times. They even offered us some sandwiches. We thanked them but told them we had some cold spaghetti waiting for us at the station.

Rodney King Riot, 1992

I was at home in Malibu one afternoon when at about 3 p.m. I received a telephone call from Capt. Tom Crewse, duty captain on the Beverly Hills Fire Department. He said they were forming a strike team to send to East LA, and that rioters were burning buildings. I had just seen the coverage on TV. He said I was needed to come in as soon as possible.

I gathered my stuff, said goodbye to my wife, and hit the road. As I was driving down the coast highway I was thinking about what I had seen on TV. The rioters had dragged this poor truck driver out of his cab and beaten him, viciously. It was hard to believe. I thought to myself, *This is going to be bad.*

As I entered the city limits of Beverly Hills I could not believe the traffic. Streets were jammed with people coming out of East LA trying to avoid the riot. I also heard this on the car radio. Over the years I've seen many traffic jams but none like this. I had to use alleys and side streets, but it still took me almost an hour to drive the last five miles to the headquarters station. I finally arrived. Capt. Crewse called a short meeting to explain our mission. We were issued bulletproof vests because reports warned that gangs were shooting at fire personnel. This was a first for me.

About this time the rest of our Strike Team 2 engine companies from Santa Monica and one engine company from Culver City arrived. We mounted up and headed for East LA. We reported into an LA station where they split up our strike team. We picked up a spotter, an LA fireman, who took our two engines to a large L-shaped mini mall with about 15 businesses, half of them in flames. We laid in our water supply from a nearby hydrant through an angry crowd and went to work on the fires. The plan was to make a stand and save the remaining businesses.

The angry crowd at our backs was calling us names and throwing anything they could get their hands on. I had never seen animosity like this toward the fire department. I was on a 1 1/2-inch hose with rookie Kerry Gardner. This situation had to be an eye-opener for him. We both had to control our emotions, because we both would have liked to turn our hose lines on the crowd, but we stayed true to our mission. We were lucky that no one in the crowd had weapons. The bulletproof vest under our turnout coat was very hot and cumbersome in this situation.

During the firefight the LA police arrived and dispersed the crowd, and we eventually extinguished the fire. Late that night the LA spotter moved us to another location, and on the way we passed city blocks on fire. We were in defense mode at this time. The fires were too big to fight with our resources, and rioters were pretty much gone, so we protected structures that were being threatened. At one point just before dawn we were moved into a large compound somewhere in East LA that looked like a fort. It was a command post, and there we received food.

We were told that some strike teams were fired upon and firemen had been injured. We were told that all strike teams would have police escorts with one cop car in front of the strike team and one in the rear as we moved to our next assignment. The sun was just starting to rise, which we could barely see because the sky was filled with black smoke, and the places we drove through looked like a war zone. Kerry and I couldn't believe what we were seeing. I looked at Kerry and said, "Well, rookie, this is just another day on the fire department. What do you think?" He shook his head and laughed.

After some more firefighting we were eventually relieved by oncoming shifts and headed for our stations where we showered, had some coffee, and told about our experience to the guys coming on. When I arrived at home my wife was glad to see me. She said it was the first time in my career that she worried about me.

She stayed up all night watching the news coverage, because they reported that gangs were shooting firemen. Several LA firemen were shot, and although they survived, they had to retire. I will never forget that day and night. It was hard to believe how people could be so stupid as to burn down their own neighborhoods. Many innocent people lost their businesses. If the rioters thought they had it tough before the riot, they would find it would be much worse after the riot.

Beverly Hills Movie Details

The City of Beverly Hills is a unique place to work in ways that are not immediately obvious. We had the very best fire and police departments in the world. The residents expect that and are willing to pay for it. One of the perks that other cities don't have is the opportunity to work on movies that are filmed throughout the city. We also have an old, stone mansion up on the hill called, Greystone Estates, set on a large number of acres that has served frequently for film making.

The city requires the film companies to take out a permit and pay a good fee to film in the City of Beverly Hills. The city also requires them to hire at least one fireman and one police officer on each day of shooting a film. The police are hired for crowd and traffic control and curfew regulation enforcement. The fire department ensures the movie set is safe and makes sure the film company follows all of the permit regulations. The fireman dressed in his uniform and working on his day off carries a radio on the set to call for paramedics or fire engine if needed.

Names of fire personnel are placed on a list so that when a movie permit is issued, you are called from this list to accept or not accept the assignment on your day off. The work pays well and is interesting most of the time. Catering companies set up to feed the film crew and anyone else assigned to the job.

I worked on at least 100 films in my 30-year career, including *The Birds, Scarface,* and *Down and Out in Beverly Hills.* It's funny how I can remember the stories I was involved in and not the films I worked on. I guess the work overall was not impressive. One thing that did amaze me was how many takes they have to shoot for one minute of film, maybe 20 to 30 takes. I often thought that if our department were that inefficient at putting out fires, the whole town would have burned down.

Lyle Slater getting some assistance from Fireman Oseguera in taking off his air tank during a structure fire in Beverly Hills late in his career

The Strangest Request

We were at the new Station 2 at around 8:30 a.m. when Capt. Cavaglieri, Engineer Hicklin, Fireman Vitali, and I had just finished a cup of coffee and some bagels. We received a chest pain call. We arrived on scene and were met by a middle-aged gentleman who explained to us that he was not having chest pains. He just wanted us there for support. He explained to us that he had received some very bad news and that he was going to have to tell his son, who was on his way over, that his young son had been killed while walking to school that morning up north. The captain said we would stay and support him.

About this time Rescue 1 arrived with paramedics Jeffrey Brown and Joe LaFirenza, better known as "Moche." The captain informed them of the situation, and they said they also would stand by until they got another call. When his son arrived at the house a few minutes later, his dad told him to sit down, and then he broke the bad news to him.

It was a terribly emotional moment for him and all of us standing there, because we all had young kids and we could relate to him and his feelings. After about 15 or 20 minutes the father received another phone call from the school, or the police, I'm not sure, that there had been a terrible identity mistake. His grandson was okay, that another boy his age had been killed. Everyone went from the lowest emotions to the highest, and then there was a short time when the son was not sure what to believe. Then he received confirmation and believed the good news. Everyone felt bad for the other boy.

We stayed there a few more minutes consoling them and then returned to the station. When we all gathered in the kitchen I explained to them I had never been on an emotional roller coaster like that, and I felt completely exhausted. They all agreed. They felt the same way, and Capt. Cavaglieri said, "Let's do the minimal housework, get the place presentable and relax, because we don't know what's in store for us the rest of the shift."

When I returned home the next morning I relayed the story to my wife. That afternoon when my kids, Suzanne and Marc, returned home from school, I gave them an extra hug and kiss.

Danny DeVito

I was home in Malibu on this beautiful day trying to do some yard work. The only problem was a Santa Anna wind blowing at 40 mph with gusts up to 60 mph. I was spending more time chasing my hat than doing yard work, so I decided to quit. As I was picking up the tools I looked up the coast and saw a large plume of black smoke blowing toward the beach. It was in the Trancus/Broad Beach area, about two miles north of my place.

I drove my pickup down to Trancus. The fire was about 1/2 mile inland at the base of the Santa Monica Mountains. I found out later that the wind blew some large branches into some power lines and downed them, and that is what started the fire. It was coming directly at me with smoke and embers flying over my head. I looked around at Broad Beach Road, which runs parallel to the coast highway and the beach where there are many expensive beach homes that belong to movie stars including Walter Matthau, Jack Lemmon, Carroll O'Connor, Pierce Brosnan, Robert Redford, Danny DeVito, and Dustin Hoffman. I could hear an LA County fire engine coming from the north from a small one-engine company about five miles up the coast and another county rig coming from the south from a fire station three miles to the south. I drove down on Broad Beach Road and picked out a house in the path of the fire that had a wood shake shingle on the roof, the very worst roof you can have on a house in a brush area.

The two houses on either side had tile and lightweight concrete for roofs. So, I parked the truck and ran up to the house and knocked on the door. A middle-aged woman opened the door, and I asked her if she were the owner, and she said, no, she was the housekeeper. The owner was in LA. I told her, "You see all the smoke? We have a brush fire coming right at us. I am an off-duty fireman, and I would like to wet the roof down to keep it from igniting."

She showed me where the garden hoses were. They were on each end of the house and looked to be 100 feet long. So, I laid them out on the windward side of the house. There was good water pressure and the nozzles were good. I took one nozzle in each hand and started to poor water on the entire roof. At times it was hard to see the entire roof because of the flying embers and smoke. Every once in a while I went around the back and wet it down, but the front roof took the biggest hit. A couple of times a large gust of wind overpowered me with a large amount of embers, and I thought the house was in trouble, but I lucked out. I had enough water and good pressure to be successful.

The engine company when they arrived attacked the main fire as it was moving toward the beach, and as more equipment arrived they got a handle on the fire in about an hour. The smoke cleared and the roof was in good shape. The housekeeper came out and said Danny DeVito owned the house, and when she informed him by phone what was going on, he asked, "Who is that superman?" I could see him saying that. That was funny. I told her I was an off-duty Beverly Hills fireman, and I lived in Malibu Park about two miles south near Point Dume. She said Danny DeVito appreciated my effort.

I returned the two hoses to their places and left. It looked like the county fire department had things under control. The next day a delivery lady arrived with a big basket of miniature cup cakes, about four dozen with a wide variety of flavors, and a thank-you note saying, "Thank you, Superman, for being so super!" It was signed, "The DeVito family." We enjoyed the cup cakes.

Beverly Wilshire Hotel Fire

I was tillering the truck about 8 p.m. when we responded to a high-rise fire at the Beverly Wilshire Hotel. When we turned west on Wilshire Blvd. we could see the fire lapping up the front of the hotel at about the fifth or sixth floors.

It was a terrible but spectacular site. Chief Bob Oliver and his driver, Jim Grove, pulled up front and they were met by a young female reporter from a local TV channel who was covering some event there. She shoved her microphone in the Chief's face and asked him, "What are you thinking, Chief?"

Chief Oliver replied, "I am thinking about the MGM fire and hope we have a better result." The reason he said that was because this was like a month after the MGM fire in Las Vegas.

The second question the reporter asked Chief was, "What is your plan?"

"I am waiting for my equipment to arrive, and when they are on scene I will send fire crews inside to the fifth floor and extinguish the fire. And now they are arriving on scene and I have to get busy."

He ordered fire crews inside to attack the fire. As the truck company pulled up he ordered us to position the truck and raised the 100-foot ariel ladder so we could use our water pipe to protect the upper floors and prevent the fire from making a run up the face of the hotel. We had one thing going for us in that the balconies partially protected that from happening. They sent me up the ladder, and when I reached the top I locked my safety belt into the ladder. I signaled Engineer Gary Poitner that I was ready for the water.

The ladder shook and twisted as water came to the nozzle. I directed the water stream above the fire, and I could see water sprays coming through the fire from the nozzles inside. In about five minutes everything went black, and then there was nothing but black smoke and steam exiting the room on the fifth floor. We were lucky. The fire did not make it into the hallway, so it was pretty much confined to one suite. The heat and smoke damaged the paint about five feet on both sides of the suite and also the suite above. The fire did look spectacular for a while.

The hotel owner was so impressed and glad to see how fast we extinguished the fire with minimal damage that he invited our shift, which was the A shift along with our wives, to a private dinner held at the hotel about a week later. I am sure the MGM Grand Hotel fire was on his mind, too. At the dinner we all enjoyed the finest wine and food money could buy. It was a very nice evening for all. My wife was impressed.

The TV coverage of the fire was on the 11 p.m. news channel, and it was also shown on the morning news, so most of the guys could see themselves in action before they left for home.

The Fourth of July

I was working at new Station 2 on Fourth of July. We had just finished lunch and were relaxing when we were dispatched to a fireworks call. Beverly Hills had a very strict fireworks ordinance banning all personal fireworks because of the fire danger. Our chief Bill Daley, along with other fire chiefs throughout the state, was working on a statewide ban of personal fireworks because of the personal danger and also the fire danger.

We responded north to the address, and when we arrived on scene we realized it was Kenny Rogers' home. It was a beautiful property set off the street quite a ways. We turned into this long beautiful driveway and drove up to the house. Captain Ron Savolskis spotted an African American man standing on the side yard.

He told us he was going over to talk to the man standing there to see what was going on. At this time the young rookie fireman Jerry Koyama started to laugh and told the captain that the man standing over there was Lionel Richie. The captain looked at him and said, "Who is Lionel Richie?" That was a funny scene.

Then we proceeded to remind him of the '84 summer Olympics that was held in LA. We told him that Lionel Richie was a very popular recording artist, and he was the main entertainment for the closing ceremonies of the '84 summer Olympics.

The captain remembered and said, "I think I will go over and talk to Lionel Richie." Ten minutes later the captain returned and said Lionel Richie was Kenny Rogers' house guest. The captain explained the ordinance to him and said Lionel Richie was very cooperative, understanding and a very nice guy. The captain did say he recognized him when he got closer.

We returned to the firehouse and had a very quiet Fourth of July. Later that evening we watched the fireworks in New York and Boston on the TV.

Four-Year-Old Child Drowning

It was late morning, and I was working at the new Station 2 with my favorite crew, Capt. Stan Speth, Engineer Renny Hicklin, and Fireman Tim Scranton when Rescue 2 received a call of a possible drowning of a small child in our district. Any life or death situation required an engine response.

So we hurriedly responded to the address which was in the most northern part of our district in the hills. We beat Rescue 2 in by three minutes and found a woman doing CPR on a four-year-old boy and a hysterical grandmother screaming, "Please save my grandson!" The grandmother we found out later was watching the child in the house and turned her back for a minute, and the child opened the screen door to the back patio and pool area. The grandmother heard a splash and realized what had happened, but by the time she was able to pull the child out of the pool, the child was unconscious. She took the child to the street which was very close and hailed down the first car, which happened to be driven by an off-duty UCLA nurse who responded by performing CPR but was having trouble doing mouth-to-mouth because the young boy had vomited. Her gag reflex was giving her problems.

We took over immediately in the entrance of the driveway. While Stan, Renny and Tim set up the equipment I wiped vomit from the child's mouth, cleared the airway and started chest compressions and mouth-to-mouth until Tim hooked up the respirator, then he took over. I continued chest compressions. At about this time the Beverly Hills Police along with Rescue 2 arrived, and the police tried to console the grandmother. That's when they got the full story from the grandmother. I felt so sorry for her.

We were doing our very best with little progress, and the decision was made by the doctors at UCLA who were in contact with Paramedic Jim Doersam to bring the patient in as fast as possible. I was appointed to drive the rescue while Tim assisted paramedics in the back compartment. Renny and Stan followed with the engine.

When we arrived at UCLA the child was hanging on but was unconscious. Eventually, he went into a coma which lasted about three weeks, and during that time I said a lot of prayers for that little one and his grandmother and parents. I also checked on his condition every shift I worked. One day I got the sad news that he had passed on. That call stuck with me, forever. I still remember it like it was yesterday, and that was some 30 plus years ago.

$500

*W*e had just finished our housework at new Station 3 where I was cooking that day, so around 11:30 a.m. we climbed aboard the engine and went shopping at Ralph's, which was in our district. I was making spaghetti with ground beef, sweet and hot Italian sausage along with garlic bread and a salad and a carrot cake for dessert.

So we did our shopping, and as we were leaving the store walking through the parking lot I looked back and saw Kerry Gardner, the other fireman, picking up something. I asked him what he was doing, and he said, "I am picking up $100 bills."

I said, "What?"

"Yes, I just picked up five $100 bills scattered around this small area."

We thought they either belonged to some old lady or were left from a drug deal. Capt. Stan Speth, Engineer Renny Hicklin, Kerry and I decided to give the $500 to the store manager and have him keep it for a week, and if no one claimed it we would be back to pick it up.

A week later Kerry called the manager who informed him that nobody had claimed the money, so Kerry got the money and decided to have a large sheet cake made and give it to the manager and his staff. Then he decided to take us all out for lunch that day at the Islands restaurant in town. We all enjoyed a nice Hawaiian meal. For the next month or so I called him "Lucky," which would bring a smile and a one finger salute.

Henry Winkler

I was working at new Station 2 one afternoon and Capt. Stan Speth was giving a class on our new airbags we had just received. The front doorbell rang, and I answered it. It was Henry Winkler with his five-year-old son. Henry asked me if I could show his son the fire engine. I said sure and invited them in for the grand tour.

We let his son try on my helmet and coat, and we put him in the engineer's seat and turned on the red lights, which he enjoyed. We figured the siren and air horn would scare him, so we didn't try it. We also gave them a tour of our living quarters, which they seemed to enjoy. We answered their questions, and they thanked us and left. On the next shift we received a large basket with four-dozen small cupcakes of all flavors from Mr. Winkler with a thank-you note saying how much they had enjoyed the fire station tour. It was our pleasure, and I think we made some new friends for the fire service. We all enjoyed the cupcakes along with some ice cream. We did leave some for the next shift.

Water Torture

I was on Engine 1 at the new headquarters station one afternoon when Capt. Speth, Engineer Larry Runyan, Fireman John Karns and I responded to an apartment building water leak call. The owner thought it was a broken water line, but after our investigation with water being splashed in our faces we determined it was a leaking sewer pipe.

We told the owner to put a bucket under the leak and call a plumber. Capt. Speth informed the watch office what we had been exposed to, UCLA Hospital Emergency was contacted, and the doctor on duty suggested we come in and get our eyes flushed.

When we arrived the nurses had us lie on three separate tables separated by curtains. We were lying on our backs face up, and they started with John. He hollered over to me, "Slater, you are going to love this." When it was my turn I saw what he meant. They taped our eyelids open and started an IV drip of water in each eye from the biggest IV bag I had ever seen. It looked like it held a gallon of water.

That was the longest hour I have ever spent in my life. When it was over we could not get the hell out of there fast enough. In the future if I ever went on another water leak call, I made sure I had my goggles on. That eye cleansing was like water torture, and I never wanted to experience that again. The treatment, however, did keep us from getting a serious eye infection. And that was good. This was just another experience in the life of a fireman.

Air Bags

On a rainy, cold evening we responded to a car accident on Coldwater Canyon north of the station. When we arrived on scene we found a Mercedes convertible resting on its top on the lawn and sidewalk.

As we approached the car Capt. Stan Speth thought the situation looked bad, but when we got to the car we were surprised to hear two people inside the car talking to each other. By this time our Rescue 1 had arrived on scene with two paramedics who asked the occupants how they were. We could not see them because of the position of a car. They were fully conscious but banged up. We told them we would get the car off of them as soon as possible. We had some new equipment airbags which were perfect for this type of rescue, but we were very nervous using them for the first time on a real rescue. We had attended classes on the equipment, but this was the real deal with lives involved.

We worked as a team and had to improvise a little. No rescue is like a classroom exercise. We were able to get the car off the ground enough to pull the two occupants out, and that was when we discovered the driver was a well-known film celebrity whose identity will be withheld.

He had lost control of the car on wet pavement and slid the car sideways into the curb going around a curve. Paramedics transported them to the emergency room to be further evaluated. Beverly Hills police took care of the car, and we returned to the station to critique our rescue. We did have some small problems with the new equipment, but we worked through them and reported the issues to the training staff.

Power Lines Down on Third Street

We had just finished cleaning new Station 2, and Capt. Casey Griffin, Engineer Larry Runyan, Firemen Kerry Gardner and I were on our way to the store to get food for the day. As we crossed Third Street I looked east down Third Street and saw a large construction crane about three or four blocks away and a bunch of arcing and sparking wires on the street. I informed the captain, and we turned around and headed down Third Street. He informed headquarters that we were responding to large voltage wires arcing and sparking on the ground and requested the power company to respond to our location ASAP.

We arrived on scene about a minute later to see four large wires arcing, sparking and whipping all over the place. I guess this crane got into the wires somehow and tore them loose. Lucky for the operator that the crane was on rubber tires, but it was hairy for a while dodging those whipping wires while trying to make the area safe. It made for good conversation over our evening meal of fried chicken which Larry prepared.

Beverly Hills Drug Brat

It was early evening. I was at the new headquarters station riding Engine 1 when we responded to a drug overdose along with Rescue 2. We arrived on scene and took our equipment into this house where we found a 14-year-old who was very obnoxious. He was acting strange and was obviously on something, which he denied. Mark Pierce, who I always thought had the best bedside manner of all our paramedics, appeared to be getting a little irritated with the kid after asking him for the fourth or fifth time what he was on.

The kid asked, "Why is my heart beating so fast?"

Mark replied, "Kid, you took something that doesn't agree with your heart. If you don't tell us what you took so we can treat you it may beat you to death."

With that statement the kid became very cooperative, and they treated and transported him to the hospital where he recovered, that time. I hope he learned a lesson, because not everyone gets a second chance.

I responded to many drug-related calls in my career, and I have never seen a good trip. If they could only see what I have seen, they would never touch mind-altering substances, whatever they may be.

Fireman's Grand Prix

A notice advertising a Fireman's Grand Prix, a charitable event to benefit a burn center, circulated around fire departments in the Southern California area. The advertisement stated that the top ten ticket sellers for this race would earn the right to go through a three-day racing school at Willow Springs, a 2.5-mile road course located in the Palmdale area. After completing the school the ten firemen would compete in the first Fireman's Grand Prix which would be a support race for the Indy Lights race a week later. The school, lodging, and most meals for the two weekends would be complimentary.

This interested me very much, because my hobby was racing. I had been racing go karts up and down the coast of Southern California for ten years. We had one month to sell as many tickets as possible, so I started selling to our firemen, businesses in town, and friends. When it was all over I was notified by the Grand Prix organization that I was the top ticket seller. So I was in!

I arrived at Willow Springs Raceway one morning to meet three racing instructors and nine other drivers from fire departments all over Southern California, a good bunch of guys. We had our orientation, and then were given new Simpson helmets with our names on them. They were donated by

Mr. Simpson, the famous safety equipment manufacturer. We also received black windbreaker jackets from Mr. Roger Penske with his racing logo on the jacket. These were very handsome jackets.

Then we went out to the garage area and were assigned a race car. These cars were slightly used Toyota Celicas with hopped up engines, roll bars installed, and race seats with 5-point harnesses like all professional race cars. The car assigned to me had Jay Leno's name on the windshield. The reason for that was that the racing school, The Driver's Connection, had contracted with Toyota to teach celebrities how to drive for the celebrity race which was a support event for the Long Beach Indy Car Race held each spring in Long Beach where they race through the city streets. Because the cars were available for the celebrities, they also were provided for the fireman's race school.

They took the celebrity names off the cars and replaced them with our names along with the fire department we were representing. We first went into the classroom for about two hours and were taught how to drive the course which was laid out on a large blackboard. They showed braking areas on each turn and enter and exit points. The cars were not automatics, so drivers had to do a lot of shifting for each turn. I had attended a go kart racing school years ago, so I was familiar with these matters except for the shifting part. Then the instructors took us out on the track for three or four laps to show us what they were telling us. The cars reached speeds of about 135 mph, and that ride was very exciting. You just don't jump in and go that fast. It took all of us a good part of that first day to slowly work our way up to that speed and feel comfortable with the car and gain confidence that the car would go through the turns at high speed. All the drivers did very well and were highly complimented by the instructors. We had some practice races on the second day, and although the cars were set up equally, some of them were a little down on power, which meant drivers had to push harder and brake later on most turns to try to make up the difference, which was my case. It was a real kick!

The weekend of the race my wife, Shirley, and I stayed at the hotel that was provided. Also staying with us were my daughter, Suzanne (who later changed her name to "Sierra Suzanne"), and son, Marc. They each brought along a friend. When we arrived at the track, we were met by some celebrities, one being Bobby Unser. He shook all of our hands and wished us well. Then they introduced us to the large crowd on hand, also mentioning the fire departments we were representing. We raced 30 laps around that 2.5-mile track. What a trip! At the end of the race all ten cars finished and were in a tight pack of about 200 feet, front to back, and I was in the middle. We all received nice trophies for participating. It was a great time. I made some good friends, the burn center received a large check, and it was good public relations for the fire service.

A year later I went to Willow Springs with my go kart for a big race. The event drew karts from all over California and surrounding states. I had never raced my go kart on a track that large. The kart weighed 150 pounds. I had a 20-horsepower engine, and the chassis rode one inch off the ground. I took that thing out there and drove it over 100 mph, which felt like 200 mph. I turned a faster time by two seconds than I had in the Toyota Celica race car a year before. The top speed of the kart was 105 mph, and the Toyota top speed was 135 mph, but the difference was that the kart went through turns like it was on rails. The Toyota had street tires, and they would slide through the turns making it pretty exciting. The G-forces on the kart with racing slicks through the turns felt like I was going to break ribs with the wrap-around seat required. I have had a lot of exciting times in my life, but this was at the top of the list, going 30 laps around Willow Springs until my engine's clutch flew off and ended my race.

Lyle Slater on his qualifying laps in his USAC TQ Midget prior to the race at Ventura Raceway in Southern California

Lyle Slater on his qualifying laps in his IMCA Modified prior to the race at Ventura Raceway in Southern California

DIVINE THUMP

Lyle Slater racing his 100-mph go kart at Saugus Speedway in Saugus, California

Lyle Slater sits on the hood of his race car prior to racing in the first Fireman's Grand Prix at Willow Springs Raceway, a 2.5-mile road course in the Southern California desert. With him is his support team from the Beverly Hills Fire Department (left to right) Captain Pettinato, Chief Cavoglieri, and Engineer Dowdle.

Transformer Explosion

I was working at the new Station 2 on a cold, rainy, foggy evening at about 10 p.m. when we received a call to respond up in the Trousdale area, the highest elevation in Beverly Hills. The call was arcing and sparking in a back yard.

Engineer Reynold Hicklin, Captain Stan Speth, Fireman Tim Scranton, and I suited up and climbed aboard the engine, and out the door we went. It was a miserable night as we turned off Sunset Boulevard and onto Trousdale, a 2 1/2 -mile steep hill. As we started to climb the hill, we ran into some fog which got thicker and thicker as we climbed. When we got to the top, visibility was almost zero. We were all straining our eyes to read any number on the curb.

We finally spotted our address and pulled up in front. We dismounted with flashlights and met a lady who was standing on her front porch. She said there was some arcing and sparking in her back yard. Tim told her that the problem was probably some circuits that got wet.

We proceeded around the side yard to the back of the house. It was so foggy we could hardly see each other a couple feet apart. As we rounded the back corner of the house we were met with this tremendous explosion and white blinding flash of light which was multiplied 10 times because of the heavy fog.

All three of us must have jumped three feet in the air. I can't say what we said when we hit the ground and our hearts started beating, again. It sounded like whatever exploded was right over our heads, and the sound about broke our eardrums. With some inspection we found out it was a transformer on a pole. The electric lines ran down the back property line and the transformer was about 40 feet above our heads. Through the heavy fog we found live wires draped over the back and side yard fences. We had come close to walking into them.

Stan called headquarters and requested the power company to respond to our location. While we waited for their arrival we had a good laugh at each other about the experience and agreed it was the loudest explosion and the brightest flash of light we had ever experienced. The power company arrived about 20 minutes later, and we turned the situation over to them to handle. We returned to the station and waited for our next experience.

Jack Lemmon

I was working at the new Station 2 one afternoon studying for an EMT re-certification test which we had to take every two years. The front doorbell rang, and it was Jack Lemmon. I let him in, and he said he was looking for an address he could not find. I took him to the apparatus room where we had a large map of the city on the wall. We could not find that address anywhere. I called Captain Stan Speth in for assistance, and he could not find it either. He called headquarters, and they could not find that address.

By this time I was thinking to myself *Jack must think we are the dumbest firemen around.* After a short time we finally decided it was the park across the street known as Coldwater Canyon Park.

Whenever we respond to something over there the dispatcher always sends us to the name Coldwater Canyon Park without any address. Jack said that is where he has to go to vote. As he left the station we imagined that he was probably thinking if we couldn't find an address across the street, how the hell could we ever find his house?

We had a few laughs about that, and every time after that when we would respond to Coldwater Canyon Park I would think of Jack Lemmon and smile.

The Bird Man of Beverly Hills

It was about 7 a.m. when Chief Daley came to work early to finish up some paperwork. As soon as he settled in he received a phone call from a peacock farmer in Iowa reporting a Pea Hen had escaped from her cage just outside of LA. The bird had flown into Beverly Hills and landed on a seventh floor ledge of a 10-story high-rise office building.

The caller said the bird had been up there for two days, and it could not live two days without water. Chief Daley did not know that someone had called in the day before and the battalion chief on duty told the caller to get in touch with the humane society. So chief Daley drove down to the scene and was confronted by a large crowd of spectators and two or three TV stations, along with three or four helicopters in the air and everyone asking him what he planned on doing about the bird.

Chief Daley said he did not want that bird to die on his watch, so he returned to headquarters and told Battalion Chief Hayes to take the truck company, on which I was the tillerman, along with Engine 3 and get that bird down safely. So the call came in over the intercom, "Bird Rescue at 8383 Wilshire Blvd," which was near our Eastern border with LA.

I had just settled down with a raisin bran muffin and a cup of coffee when Dale Nordberg, my backup Tillerman who loved getting all the experience he could tillering, asked me if he could take the call for me. I said, "Sure, go ahead," not knowing at the time I had just given away my 15 minutes of fame on national television. I asked him to transfer my equipment to Engine 5 which he was assigned to. He said he would, then slid the poll and a minute later I heard them leave the station. I enjoyed my muffin and coffee.

I heard this story when they returned: When the truck company arrived on scene they were met with a large crowd and the bird owners who supplied them with two five-foot poles with a large net attached to the end of each pole. The truck crew had a problem. They could not use the aerial ladder to reach the bird because of the large setback of the building which prevented them from getting close enough. They tried a few other options that did not work.

So they took all of their repelling equipment to the roof, and then they had another problem. They could not send two guys over the side and repel down on their own because they needed both hands free to operate the poll and net. So Dale Nordberg and Dave Gonzales were the two guys appointed to go over the side. They tied a 300-foot rope to Dale and Dave's safety belt, and with four strong firemen holding on to each rope, they assisted Dale and Dave over the side of the building and gingerly lowered them down the face of the building toward the bird on the window ledge. They were about ten feet apart positioned to come down on each side of the window.

This preparation took quite a bit of coordination between the chief on the ground who was in radio communication with the guys on the roof observing and lowering them in to position. When they reached the seventh-floor window the bird was closest to Dale, so he put his net in place, and Dave after a couple tries was able to coax the bird into Dale's net like it was a common event, which it was not. This had never been done by our department.

Dale, who was very muscular, grabbed the bird. He had a death grip on the bird, and Dave, who was a little concerned, told Dale to ease up a little. If they were to kill that bird on national TV, it would not look good. Dale relaxed a little and secured the bird in the net. They were lowered to the ground safely with much fanfare from the large crowd. They handed the bird over to the grateful owners, and then they had many microphones shoved in their faces, forcing them to answer many questions. We all heard the answers back at the station on the evening news.

This type of rescue was a first for us, and it goes to show you never know what to expect when you come to work in this profession. That's what makes firefighting so challenging and interesting. That night Dale received a call from his mother in Chicago. Her friend had seen him on TV in Chicago and told her to catch it on the next news broadcast, which she did.

When Dale first came on the department, for some reason I always called him "Dale Bird." It just sounded good, and he didn't mind it, but from that time on I called him "the bird man of Beverly Hills," and Dale would respond by saying, "Lyle man, the man who gave me my 15 minutes of fame"

Car Fire on Wilshire Boulevard

I was working with my old buddy Chuck Oseguera at new Station 3 one evening when at around 9 p.m. we responded to a car fire on Wilshire Boulevard in the northeast end of our district. As we made a right-hand turn from Doheny onto Wilshire Boulevard Capt. Carl Urman said we had a real Ripper. Chuck and I looked down about five blocks and saw what he was talking about, a big red glow on the north side of the street.

As we pulled up in front of a car that was half on the street and half on the sidewalk, we could see that the car was fully involved in fire. A police officer informed the captain that two men were inside. We jumped into action. I took the pre-connected 1 1/2-inch tank line off the engine and stuck it into the passenger compartment on the driver side with a three-quarter fog pattern and whipped it around for about a minute until the fire was extinguished. I attacked next the engine compartment by using a full fog and pushing the hose and nozzle back and forth under the engine compartment. In the meantime Chuck and the captain were extracting the two badly-burned bodies out of the car.

At about this time Rescue 1 arrived on scene. Because we had two critical patients, they called for Rescue 2. The driver was alive, but the passenger had no pulse. Chuck and

I assisted Rescue 1 in doing CPR on the passenger, and the captain and the engineer assisted the driver until Rescue 2 arrived a few minutes later.

Rescue 1 Paramedic Mark McNicoll was calling the shots and was in contact with UCLA Hospital. When we stabilized the patients the best we could, we loaded them up for a fast drive to UCLA. I drove Rescue 1 and Chuck drove Rescue 2. The passenger was pronounced dead at the hospital. The driver did survive, although badly burned.

The story of what happened on this call was told to Capt. Urman by an LA cop. He said they chased the two guys who were driving a stolen vehicle into Beverly Hills at high speeds, and they collided with a tow truck where the perpetrators lost control of their vehicle and rolled the car. It landed on the sidewalk on its wheels and burst into flames. Police used a dry chemical fire extinguisher with little effect. The Beverly Hills police were also on the scene when we arrived, and I assumed they were the ones who called us.

Months later some of us were subpoenaed to testify who was the driver, because the driver who survived claimed he was not the driver. This was important because the driver was being charged for the death of the passenger. I was lucky. I was on a motor home trip across the country with my wife, Shirley, my daughter, Sierra Suzanne, and my son, Marc, for 54 days during this time and did not have to appear in court.

It Never Rains in California

*I*n 1992 California for weeks experienced torrential rain storms caused by El Niño. I was working at headquarters assigned to tillering on Truck 4. The rain just poured down, and our department was very busy with roof leaks, minor flooding, and car accidents. Then we responded to a flooding in late afternoon at the intersection of Wilshire Boulevard and La Cienega which was on the eastern side of Beverly Hills.

As we were nearing that intersection about a half a block away Engineer Gary Poitner said over the intercom, "Holy cow! We have some water here!" We encountered about a foot of water at first, then as we reached the intersection of Wilshire and La Cienega, water ran above our running boards well over two feet deep, and we found about a dozen cars floating in all directions as all of our fire equipment arrived along with the police personnel. We started to rescue the people in the cars.

We either pushed the cars to shallow water where they could take off on their own, or we walked people out to shallow water. We had to make sure we didn't fall into any of the storm manholes which had been blown off because of the overloaded storm drain system. If we had fallen into any of them, we would have been washed out to sea some 15 miles or so away.

We had some high-rise buildings in this area with subterranean garages full of cars, and they were all submerged in water. What a mess! I was teamed up with Joe Radish through this whole operation, and when we had everybody cleared out of the intersection Joe and I walked one block east through 2 1/2 feet of water. We heard an explosion.

A car in the subterranean garage of a fairly large apartment building floated into a gas meter and broke the pipes. Gas found an ignition point and blew up part of the first floor killing an elderly lady. The fire department along with the city workers were trying desperately to turn the gas off, but it was hard to find the gas shut off in the street because of at least two feet of water in the area. The building was evacuated, and responders were eventually able to find a shut off and evacuate the deceased lady's body.

It was a long afternoon and evening before we returned to the station. We ate a very late supper. I was told the reason we had had a flood in this area for the first time since I had been working for the department was that when the city was built many years ago, the eastern part of the city was built in a wash which drained a lot of water from the Hollywood Hills to the north of the city. The storm system installed then was able to handle it until the 100-year rains or El Niño's hit which overwhelmed the sewer system.

After this event storm sewers were upgraded to handle this type of situation in the future, and to my knowledge they have never had a problem since.

Slater's Ariel Act

Firefighters as a whole are active people, so on their days off they are involved in all types of sports. While most of the firemen on my departments were involved in golf, dirt bike riding and water sports, my interests were in race cars.

When I was 11, 12, and 13 years old I was involved in the Cleveland Ohio Soap Box Derby. My brother, Dick, and I were both champions. I remember pulling a chair up to a large console radio and listening to the entire Indianapolis 500 race. I would be the first in the car when my dad would take Dick and me, along with friends, to our local race track.

Years later when I was on the Beverly Hills Fire Department and 45 years old I started to race go karts, then midgets and IMCA modifieds up and down the California coast. I raced with Bryon Hurda and Ricky Hurn before they became well known. I also raced midgets on Saturday nights at Ventura Raceway with Jay Drake, Cory "the cruiser" Crusman, and Jason Leffler, who I am sorry to say was killed in a sprint car crash as I was writing this.

When I was racing midgets I would always take some of my fireman buddies with me to help me prepare the race car. One Saturday night I had John Karns and Bruce Maurer with me for the first time. They were in the grandstands, and I was on the track in a heat race. It was the second lap going about 85 mph down the back straight going into turn three when the guy on my right, John Sarna, who was about a half car ahead of me, decided to turn left.

He ran over the nose of my car, and I remember seeing his front number panel, then I saw nothing but dirt, sky, lights, crowd, dirt, sky, lights, and crowd. Everything was spinning in front of me. My car did seven flips end over end in about the time it would take to say, "Oh, crap!" which I did say every time the car hit the ground. It felt like someone was hitting me on both shoulders with a sledgehammer. I was thinking to myself *when the hell is this thing going to stop?* It was a good thing my crew pulled my belts extra tight when I got in.

When it finally did stop and the safety crew arrived I was upside down, and I was not responsive for a minute or so. They turned the car upright and assisted me out of the car. The crowd cheered and acknowledged they were happy that I was able to walk away.

The car was destroyed. The front end was torn off, all four wheels bent and hanging on the two axles, which were also bent. The fuel cell was folded up to my seat but did not break. The drive shaft was torn out of the rear end, and the crank in the engine was bent. The steering wheel which I had a death grip on was bent up about four inches from normal.

I had angels riding with me that night for sure. My two buddies told me later that prior to knowing the outcome they thought they would have to tell my wife Shirley that I got killed.

The announcer and race promoter, Jim Naylor, stopped by in the pits later and said, "Slater, don't ever do that again. You almost gave me a heart attack."

I said, "I don't plan on doing that again."

People stopped by in the pits after the race to say they were happy I was okay. They said it was the worst TQ (3/4 midget) crash they had ever seen. A film maker was at the track that night and made me a video and a collage of eight pictures of the car in different positions as I flew through the air. He called it "Slater's Ariel Act."

When Shirley, who was normally at the track but not this night, saw the video she said she was glad she had not been there to see it.

I had a headache for two days due to a slight concussion, and my neck and shoulders were sore for a week. That was it. This was August of 1993. I was out of racing for the rest of the season, which ended six weeks later.

I did not know it at the time, but this was to be my last midget race. In November of 1993 I was involved in the worst brush fire to hit Malibu in recent memory and came down with a heart problem due to exposure to heavy smoke. At the end of that year, they retired me from the Beverly Hills Fire Department.

This was a big life change for me. I was out of the job I loved, firefighting, and out of the sport I loved, racing.

Two Million to One Chance

One November day in 1993 I was working at the new headquarter station. There were maybe 10 brushfires burning in Southern California. The Santa Ana winds were blowing, and every department was either on standby or already working on these fires. I was a crew member on Engine 1 along with Capt. Eddie LaFouge, Engineer Chuck Beagle, and Fireman Jeffrey Nolan.

    LA County called us at about 2 p.m. for a strike team. Our strike team was made up of two engine companies from Beverly Hills, two from Santa Monica, and one from Culver City, and our chief, Bob Cavaglieri, and his driver, George Richards. LA County said they had a brush fire in Moorpark that had just broken out, and they needed our help. Moorpark was about 30 miles northwest of Beverly Hills. The strike team gathered at our headquarters, and we responded with red lights and siren to Moorpark. We arrived around 4 p.m. The fire was up in the hills and not threatening any structures. The wind seemed to die down. We decided that this might be a good time to get some fast food, because we were not sure when we would get another chance. That was a good idea, because we never got another chance to eat until mid-afternoon the next day.

There was a Wendy's restaurant nearby, so we all got hamburgers and soft drinks. When we were finished a spotter met us and took us to our assignment. The wind had picked up by now and was blowing toward a new subdivision. This was the first time in my 30-year career that we were in front of the fire and not chasing it. Because of this we had a short time to set up and wait for it and plan our attack. We were very lucky that this was a new subdivision with Class A roofs and stucco exteriors. The residents also had cleared the brush around the perimeter of the subdivision, so we were basically left with trees and bushes that would be our problem.

Our engine company was assigned two houses, so we laid out our hoses accordingly. We had good water pressure. Most of the residents were evacuated. A few decided to stay. We looked around for obvious things that might catch fire easily and took care of them. California was in a five-year drought, so everything was very dry, and this area had not burned in a long time. The fire load was very heavy. When the fire came at us, we had a 50-foot wall of flame to contend with, but we were lucky because of the clearance. Trees and bushes were threatened because of all the flying embers. It was like being in a huge rainstorm of flying embers with a 70-mph wind pushing them horizontal to the ground.

We were challenged to stay on our feet. We sprayed every bush and tree around the houses to keep them from exploding in flames. We were pretty successful with our efforts, and after the fire blew by we continued to put out small fires around the houses. We stayed there all night doing this, and when daylight broke all the houses were standing with very little damage. All of the vegetation, however, was charred to an ugly black and gray ash. About this time everything was under control, and after we picked up our hose lines we were told to go to a local park for breakfast where they had a portable kitchen.

When we arrived at the park and before we could get off the rigs we were told we had to respond to Malibu some 20 miles away, because the fire that we had just fought was heading straight for the northwesterly end of Malibu and threatening homes and small ranches. Our strike team headed west with red lights flashing and sirens blaring. When we hit the coast highway and headed towards Malibu the fire was chasing deer off the mountainside and some of them were landing on the pavement in front of us, a terrible site. We headed up a winding canyon road that the fire had not reached and were assigned to protect some scattered houses. Our engine company was assigned a small five-acre ranch to protect. We had enough time to set up our equipment and lay out our hose lines to protect a small ranch house and the horse barn.

A private hydrant on the property would provide plenty of water. The fire was about a half mile away and was expected to arrive in about ten minutes. We released five horses in the barn to a 200-foot square dirt corral, because if the barn were to catch fire we did not want to have to deal with the horses under those conditions. Then we took our air tanks off the rig and put them up against a post in the center of the dirt corral.

If all hell were to break loose, this was our safe zone. We had one big problem. The property had tall pine trees on the east side of the house and along the 300-foot driveway that passed near the barn. We had to keep the fire out of these trees or we could lose everything. So we laid out our hose accordingly. When the fire hit we were ready for it, but what we weren't ready for was that the fire split and went around the corral to the west and headed for the trees near the barn. The other part of the fire came around the east side of the house toward the pine trees. We spent the better part of an hour running from one end of the property to the other end knocking the fire down around the trees before it got a good hold on them. We would knock the fire down at one end, run to the other end to do the same and then back again. At 54 years old and with 30 years on the job, I experienced the hardest work ever on this fire, but we were successful in saving the barn and house and most of the trees and the horses.

After we picked up our equipment we were so hungry we went into the house which was evacuated and found a loaf of bread and some peanut butter and jam along with some sodas. This was the best lunch I ever had. The captain left a brief note of thanks, and we left to go to our next assignment.

Our next assignment was to protect two houses that were on a narrow ridge line which had fire coming at it from the northeast. A narrow road or large driveway about 500 feet long led up to the houses with no place to turn around, so the whole strike team of five engine companies backed down to the houses for a quick getaway if and when we had to leave. We only had 500 gallons of water in each rig, so we were limited. I was dropped off at the intersection of the driveway and the street to provide fire watch. This ridge was a very dangerous place to be in a brush fire for the whole strike team. I was left there with a radio and told if the embers flew over the house and fell into the canyon on the southwesterly side of the driveway and I could see fire, to call immediately so we could pull out before we were between two fires burning up both sides of the canyon.

The wind was blowing about 70 mph, and I had a hard time standing. I had a very good vantage point from where I was standing to see everything I could through the blinding smoke. The five engine companies were hard at work. I heard some voices behind me, turned around and was surprised to see a news crew getting ready to film. I was surprised because this was not a safe place. They must have figured that because we were there they were safe. They were wrong if that's what they thought, because no one was safe there. They asked me what I was doing, and I told them I was a fire watch, and as soon as the embers flew into the canyon we were going to get the hell out of there, and they had better run, too.

We were there maybe one half hour when embers began to fall into the canyon, and I was having a hard time seeing through the smoke. I saw a red glow at the bottom of the canyon, and I radioed, "This is the fire watch. We have fire in the canyon." I repeated that message two or three times, and I began to see some activity around the rigs and knew they were getting ready to evacuate. The fire was racing up the canyon when they started to pull out. Casey Griffin was the captain on the first rig out and as he passed me he said, "Good job, Slater, and let's get the hell out of here!" I climbed onto the second engine out.

The whole strike team made it to the street. I looked back to see that the area where the strike team had been parked five minutes earlier now was on fire. I thought the only chance those two houses had was that they were low enough, and the fire because of the steepness of the canyon would blow over the top of them. We headed down the canyon road where at one point the fire was getting close to the road. We found a large area where they had cleared maybe a 300-foot square area for a new house, so we pulled in there for safe refuge and prepared ourselves to take on a lot of heat and flying embers, which came very soon. We stayed in our rigs, which were not fully enclosed, and the other fireman, Jeff Nolan, and I were in the jump seats which were partially covered. We took out our fire shelters (aluminum blankets) and used them to protect us from the heat and embers. When the fire blew by everyone was okay.

We moved to another location where we met our relief personnel from Beverly Hills. Brett Wilson and Glenn Pinson were Jeff's and my relief. They pulled up in two fire prevention cars and came over to us. Brett said, "You guys look like you have had it."

I said, "Welcome to hell. We've been there and back." Glenn asked about the deployed fire shelters, and I told them the story. They informed us that we should get down the canyon road to the Pacific Coast Highway as quickly as possible to prevent being cut off by the fire which was heading that way. After turning things over to them we high-tailed it out of there, made it to the coast highway and headed for Beverly Hills about 1 1/2 hours away.

As we drove down the coast I thought to myself *I finally feel like we did all we could to save structures. Our strike team did not lose any homes. I felt we had done a great job,* although there were 268 homes lost in the total fire.

I did not know I had just fought my last brushfire. I had not been feeling up to par after the fire because of the heavy smoke I had inhaled for two days. On 30 December 1993 after a strenuous rescue call while working out of Station 2, I experienced back and chest pains. I had a bad cold, and I thought I might be coming down with bronchitis. Chief Cavaglieri was visiting our station, and I told him and Capt. Stan Speth to get somebody to take my place that evening, that I wanted to go to Kaiser and be checked out for back and chest pain. The chief told me to sit down, and he called for the paramedics.

The paramedics checked me out and decided to take me straight to Cedars-Sinai Hospital. I called my wife to tell her what was happening, and I told her she might have to cancel our New Year's plan to stay in a bed and breakfast near Santa Barbara. At Cedars they determined that I had a 95 and a 99 percent blockage in my main arteries. I was close to having a heart attack. On 2 January 1994 they did an angioplasty on both arteries.

Shortly after that they retired me ending my 30 years as a fireman. Six months later one of the arteries closed and had to be reopened. Four months after that the same artery closed down, again, and they reopened it. At that time they told me to look for a good heart surgeon, because if the artery were to close down again a bypass would be in order.

So I started asking our paramedics and friends if they knew a good heart surgeon. Then one day while I was at my dentist in Malibu, he recommended I see a retired heart surgeon from Cedars who lived across the street from him. So I did. This retired doctor said if he were to have a bypass, he would have Dr. Scholl from Cedars-Sinai Hospital perform the operation. So I had a name and was in the process of contacting him.

In the meantime, one morning my wife and I went up the coast to Neptune's Net, a surfer hangout near the Malibu and Ventura City line for breakfast. This was about a year after my last brush fire. When we finished breakfast Shirley said she would like to see the area where we had fought the fire a year ago. We drove up to the ranch that we had protected, and I told her how we had fought the fire. We saw a For Sale sign on the property. We had been looking for a place with more property then the acre and a half we had in Malibu Park, so we decided to drive in and talk to the owners.

An elderly gentleman dressed in a T-shirt and bib overalls answered the door. I told him we had seen the For Sale sign and were interested in looking at the property. I then asked him if he had owned the property a year ago when the fire came through. He said he had, and I told him I was one of four guys who protected his property. He was so glad to hear this that he invited us in, that he along with his wife wanted to hear all about the fight to protect his property. I told him how we fought the fire and the problems we had and thanked him for the peanut butter jelly sandwiches. He laughed, and then he and his wife took us for a walk around the property.

While we were walking, my wife was up front with the gentleman, and his wife and I were about 15 feet behind. The owner's wife asked me if I were still a fireman, and I told her they had retired me with a heart problem a year ago, and that I might need a bypass. She wanted to know which hospital I was going to, and when I said Cedars she informed me that her husband worked there as the head cardiac surgeon. When I asked his name she said Dr. Scholl. I about fell over. I hollered to Shirley, "You will never guess who you are walking with. That's Dr. Scholl." She about fell over. That had to be a two million-to-one chance that with ten brushfires burning at the time we were dispatched to the Malibu fire, that I would be on a four-man crew protecting his house, and he would be on a team of doctors at Cedars that may have to perform my heart bypass a year later. That was a very special moment. We explained to him and his wife that he was the doctor recommended to us. He informed us he would be happy to perform the bypass if I needed it, so that was settled.

About a month later I was running on the sand at Broad Beach in Malibu not far from my house, and I experienced chest pain of about one on the scale of 10. I informed my cardiologist, and he said bring your heart surgeon in and we will do an angiogram. So this was performed at Cedars and Dr. Scholl was there shoulder to shoulder with the doctor performing the angiogram. After it was done they came out and told my wife there was no blockage, that everything look good, and Dr. Scholl had no idea why I was experiencing that pain. He told her not to worry. Only because it was Dr. Scholl saying so she did not worry. That was 18 years ago. I still get my six-month checkup twice a year and never have had a heart problem since. This story is another reason why I think someone has been guiding me or looking after me. That was a two million-to-one chance that would happen.

Christmas Time at the Waldorf

My daughter, Sierra Suzanne, lived in New York with her husband, Phil, in a two-bedroom apartment across the street from Central Park. We were there to spend Christmas with them along with our son, Marc, who would be staying with them. Shirley wanted to stay at the Waldorf which was beautifully decorated at Christmas time, and so we did.

My daughter and son joined us for the day, and we went to Central Park and enjoyed a special gift from my daughter, a horse-drawn carriage ride through Central Park in the snow.

One of the days while going out to eat in one of the fine restaurants in the area, we walked through the beautiful lobby of the Waldorf and past two large portraits. They were about four feet by eight feet and were of Conrad Hilton and his son. As we passed the pictures, my wife commented to me, "Just think, you saved Conrad Hilton's great grandchildren." I was surprised, because I did not know they owned the Waldorf Astoria.

I asked, "Did you know that they owned this hotel?"

She said, "Yes."

I smiled at Shirley and said, "You always have been smarter than I am."

As I walked out of the lobby, I had a little spring to my step. There were many dignitaries over the years who had stayed at the Waldorf Astoria, but none could claim to have saved the great grand children of Conrad Hilton.

Nine Eleven

I looked at the clock as I rolled over in bed. I was surprised to see that I had slept until 10 a.m. As I got dressed looking from our second-story master bedroom, I could see it was a picture-perfect day in Malibu. I looked out over a green field to a beautiful dark blue ocean 1/2 mile away. It was such a clear day I could see the Channel Islands about 40 miles away.

 I was excited about today because my daughter, who my wife, Shirley, and I have not seen for about a year, was flying to LAX from JFK in New York and would be with us that afternoon. We would take her to a nice lunch before returning to Malibu. I went downstairs and as I rounded the corner going into the dining room I looked down into the family room and saw the TV was on showing a large high-rise fire. I thought to myself, *That's one hell of a fire.*

 I called for Shirley with no answer. I went into the kitchen, called again, and she answered from the garage which was off the kitchen. I could tell her voice sounded like she was sobbing. I found her sitting on a small step with her back to the washer and dryer and a phone in her hand, crying. I asked her what was wrong. She asked if I had seen the TV. I said yes, that there was a large high-rise fire burning. She said Marc, our son, had called and asked if she had seen the TV. She turned it on, then our son-in-law, Phil, called from New York, very disturbed, saying Sierra Suzanne's plane had taken off 15 minutes before a large plane flew into one of the twin towers, and he thought that plane might be the one she was on, because news outlets were reporting that the plane that hit the tower was bound for California.

My wife said, "Hearing this, I felt like my heart was torn out of my chest. I have never experienced that sadness in my life."

I asked her how long she had been dealing with this and why she had not awakened me. She said Marc had called about an hour and a half ago, and because of my heart problem she did not want me to be involved until she found out for sure what had happened. I can't tell you what a depressed feeling I had at that moment. It was terrible. We went back into the house and down into the family room where the TV was, and they were reporting that a second plane had flown into the other tower. They were saying it was a terrorist attack.

About 15 or 20 minutes later we received the best call we have ever received. It was from Sierra Suzanne. She said, "Mom, we're going to be a little late. We had an emergency with the plane according to the captain, and we have landed in Cincinnati, Ohio. I'm not sure what's happening. A lot of people are upset and crying."

I got on the phone, and Shirley and I expressed how elated we were to hear her voice. I told her, "You don't have a problem with the plane. The U.S. has a big problem. We have been hit by terrorists flying planes into buildings, and we are so relieved and happy you weren't on those planes."

We kept telling her how overjoyed we were that she was okay. "You can't believe what your mother went through for a couple of hours. We went from the lowest to the highest feelings of joy a parent can experience." I told her to get into a hotel closest to the airport as fast as possible. "All planes in the U.S. are grounded, and every person on a plane is going to be stranded. Hotels will fill up fast." She hung up and called back a few minutes later saying she had gotten a room at the Sheraton Hotel at the airport.

I told her I would call my brother who lived in Medina, Ohio, about 40 miles southwest of Cleveland, and have him pick her up. It would be about a six-hour drive. I called my brother, Dick Slater, and told him where Sierra Suzanne was. He picked her up, and she stayed with him for three days trying to get a plane out of Cleveland Hopkins Airport for LA with no luck, so she decided to rent a car and head west staying in touch with her cell phone.

The next day my wife and I headed east with our cell phone on to stay in contact with Sierra Suzanne. We met in Vail, Colorado, where she was able to secure two adjoining rooms in a plush hotel.

Shirley and I could see the hotel off in the distance, but because of the one-way streets, we were having a hard time getting there even though Sierra Suzanne was trying to direct us on her cell. It was becoming frustrating until our "Angel," as we called him, appeared in his old truck with American flags stuck all over the bed and windows. He asked us if we needed any help. We told him we were trying to get to that hotel over there where we were going to meet our daughter who had just driven cross country from Ohio. He said, "I'll show you the way. Follow me."

I cannot begin to express the feelings Shirley and I had following that truckload of American flags waving in the breeze through the maze of small streets until we saw the hotel where Sierra Suzanne was staying. It was surreal!

When we pulled into the parking lot, and I saw our daughter running toward us, it was the best sight my wife and I had ever seen. That was quite an emotional rendezvous.

I thanked the guy in the truck, called him an angel and asked him what he was going to do with all the flags. He said, "You see that mountain over there? Tomorrow morning I'm going to put them all on that outcropping up there." I told him they would look fantastic up there.

Sierra Suzanne, Shirley and I enjoyed a nice evening together over a great dinner with plenty of wine. The next day we turned her car in to the rental agency and headed for Malibu where we enjoyed each other and had a fantastic visit together for three or four weeks.

About six months later my wife and I visited Sierra Suzanne in New York City. She and her husband now lived in a nice apartment near Gramercy Park. While I was there I took a day by myself and visited Ground Zero where the towers once stood. It was quite a sight to see all the flowers, pictures and notes left on the fence surrounding the area.

I also visited a four-man fire station about half a mile from Ground Zero. The men stationed there said the four men who were in quarters on 9/11 were among the first on the scene that day, and because they were in good shape, they were probably the highest crew in the first tower when it came down. They said they never found them or their equipment. It was like they were vaporized. The four firemen left behind 16 children ranging from six months to 16 years of age.

The crew working there on that day was friendly, but you could tell they had gone through hell losing so many friends. It was as though they had the spirit of life sucked out of them. When I first got on the department I experienced that feeling to some degree when we lost four firemen and a pilot on a hunting trip in a plane crash. I attended five funerals in a very short period of time. I could not imagine losing as many friends as each one of them had in a couple of hours.

I felt so bad for them that as I was getting ready to leave I wrote a check to give to the captain for the four families who lost their loved ones. The captain asked me if I would care to join them for lunch, and I said it would be an honor. I was treated to the best New York hamburger and fries along with some homemade tomato soup. It was great.

When I left there I visited the headquarters station that was near Ground Zero. It was a station where two French filmmakers were making a film about a rookie. When 9/11 happened they made a documentary of the event. While I was there I saw a large wall in the station with about 781 names on it of all the firemen who had died in the line of duty since the Fire Department of New York was established in 1865. To put the terrorist event in perspective, on 9/11 in New York City the fire department lost almost half of the 781 firefighters lost in 136 years, 343 lives lost on 9/11 in less than two hours. That is how devastating 9/11 was to New York. Unbelievable.

That Christmas my daughter and son-in-law spent Christmas with us in Malibu. They gave me a large book of the New York Fire Department and the 9/11 tragedy along with a statue of a fireman and angel. I looked through the book and I saw all the stations and all the men's faces who gave their lives that day. I started to tear up. My daughter noticed and said, "Dad, don't you like the book?"

I said, "I love the book. You could not have given me anything better, but it brought back memories of that day when we thought we had lost you, and then for the first time seeing all the faces of those brave men it bought it home to me for the first time that I lost 343 brothers that day. You see, all firemen are members of a large brotherhood, and these guys were not only brothers but my heroes."

It was an emotional moment.

Blessings in Disguise

Shirley and I visited her cousin, Jim Green, and his wife, Tammy, in Florida in 2013. While we visited them we were introduced to a neighbor, Bill Bresnan, who is a retired New York firefighter. We exchanged a few stories, and one of his stories was similar to an experience I had early in my career. The similarity in experience and the outcomes are worth sharing. The stories are about two firemen working on opposite sides of the country going for a promotion and not getting it, which turned out to be blessings in disguise.

My story started about half way through my rookie year. I was working with Capt. Comer at old Station 3. Capt. Comer was the oldest and most experienced captain on the job. He spent a lot of time teaching me everything a rookie fireman should know. One day Capt. Comer received a call from Battalion Chief Jackson instructing him to start teaching me how to become an acting engineer. Rookies normally are not trained to be acting engineers, and the captain expressed this to him. The chief said, "If you and the engineer, Vern O'Coner want to go on vacation this year, Slater will be your acting engineer."

The captain started teaching me hydraulics and the duties on how to maintain the fire engine. We also did a lot of driving, and I had to study and remember the streets and running lanes in Engine 3 district. It was a lot to learn in a short time, but the captain was a good teacher, and I was able to accomplish it.

So I drove the engine when our engineer and our captain were off duty. When that happened, the regular engineer would act as captain. Later on when I moved to other stations, I did the same when called upon. Eventually, I was qualified to take the engineer's test. I was not interested in making Engineer my permanent occupation. The captain's job is what I was really interested in, but I thought being a captain you should have the experience of the engineer job so when you would be in charge of a crew and had to tell the engineers what to do, you would know what you were talking about. So I studied for the engineer's test, and I made the list. Because I had no seniority, I was fourth or fifth on the list like it should be. The more senior you were, you should have that advantage. The list lasted two years, and in that two-year period, only two openings became available, and I "died on the list," as they called it.

I was still disappointed, and about the time the next test rolled around two years later, I was studying very hard for it. Then I noticed the captain's job was changing. Responsibilities were added to the job such spending two years working 8 a.m. to 5 p.m. as a training officer making out training plans and giving classes. That was not for me. I liked working a 24-hour shift, and as far as giving classes, I always said I would rather fight ten guys than give a class to ten guys.

After that was over, a captain candidate had to become a fire marshal and spend two years working another 8 a.m. to 5 p.m. job going to schools, giving talks, doing arson investigations, and following up inspections with a lot of paper work. Again, not for me. So if I had made the engineer's job, I would have been stuck there because of the changes in the captain's job, meaning I would be out in the street twisting dials and not where the action was. I would not have experienced the calls in this book, including having a hand at saving 22 people's lives, because I would have been on different shifts, on different days. I would have been unhappy in that job. So staying a fireman, I experienced everything in this book and much more, and I loved every minute. So thank you, God, for your guidance.

The next story, written by New York retired firefighter, Bill Bresnan, reveals his blessing in disguise when he was passed over for promotion late in his career.

Bill Bresnan's Blessing in Disguise

It was sometime during the year 2000 when the results of the lieutenant's test for the Fire Department of New York came out. The original answer key came out on the night following the actual test. The answer key was sent out over the computer to all the firehouses as potential officers awaited their fate. I had full seniority and some awards for meritorious acts including a medal for a rescue made in the crater during the first attack on the World Trade Center in February of 1993. The crater was a huge blown-out section in the below-surface parking area with so many supports destroyed that there was a big concern about the stability of the building.

All I had to do was pass the test, and my seniority and awards would move me up the list.

I did not like the test, because many questions were not complete, or rather, the answers were not complete. In other words, you couldn't really answer the question based on any one of the multiple choice answers. Two of the choices were necessary for a complete answer in many cases, but you were asked to give the BEST answer.

For example, there was a question about taxpayers (one-story buildings such as stores, which were basically built to pay the taxes on the property). The question went something like, "You are the officer of a tower ladder (as opposed to an aerial ladder) and are first to arrive at a taxpayer fire. You would direct the chauffer [engineer] to place the tower ladder a) in front of the building b) the long side of the building c) (I forget what c was) or d) (I forget what d was)." Answers c) and d) are not important in this illustration, because we're only concerned with answers a) and b).

The books say that a tower ladder has priority for the front of the building if the fire is in a taxpayer, and that's where the truck should be. It also says to take the long side of the building, if possible. Sometimes the long side of the building is all brick. You want the area that is most exposed (glass). It just so happens that with many of these taxpayers, such as grocery stores, the front of the building *is* the long side. That's where the check-out counters are, etc. The answer they were looking for was b) the long side of the building. I chose a) because it was the BEST answer.

So when you take a test such as this, you become frustrated, because you know the material and they're not giving you what you need to properly answer the question.

They've been known to screw around with tests. I know of a chief's test (which only captains are eligible to take) where they wanted you to pretend you were the chief of an imaginary fire department. They wanted you to forget the procedures you knew that are used in the New York City Fire Department, and they would give you their own set of procedures and require you to direct companies and operations using their set of rules. (I guess this was some sort of clever way to measure a man's inherent ability for decision making.)

Anyway, getting back to the lieutenant's test, as it turned out after the answer key came down, I had passed the test and was excited about becoming a lieutenant. I envisioned myself in a new, fancier uniform that had two rows of buttons, silver stripes on the sleeves with some cool medallions on the lapels and a white hat. My wife even ordered a special watch for me.

However, they made changes to the test, sixteen to be exact, after I took the test. It took a whole year to promulgate the list, and I ended up with a 72, but needed a 73 to pass. I missed becoming a lieutenant by one point. I was broken hearted, and there was nothing I could do about it except wait for the next test which wouldn't be for another four years. I became angry and resentful, and since I had twenty years on the job and was eligible for retirement, I chose to walk my retirement paper through the battalion and division. My retirement date was July 25, 2001.

Less than two months later, on September 11, 2001, the Trade Center was attacked, and my company was one of the first to respond. Fourteen men from my firehouse were killed.

Each year I hear their voices talking on the handi-talkies when the History Channel shows footage of the events of 9/11. I knew at least fifty of the men who were killed. Needless to say, I will never forget them. It is something you never really recover from.

I think of them often and remember the good times we had, the smiles, the laughter, and the crazy firefighting experiences we shared.

I also feel a good amount of guilt that I lived and they did not.

Had I gotten one more question right on the lieutenant's test, I would have been waiting to get promoted and would have been working that day. One more question would have cost me my life.

I'm not sure about fate, or that things happen for a reason. I could have studied harder, joined a study group, attended fire tech (a classroom environment to help students review the many thousands of items of information necessary to pass the lieutenant's test), but I didn't.

I have taken many more breaths and enjoyed the beauty of this earth for many more days than my fallen brothers.

God Bless them and their families, and God Bless America.

—-Bill Bresnan, Ladder # 15, FDNY, *Retired*

Lyle and Shirley Slater visited the Beverly Hills Fire Department in July of 2012.

A Great Run

I am sitting in a comfortable chair in the Commonwealth Cancer Center of Kentucky receiving chemotherapy to treat Myelodesplastic Syndromes (MDS), a blood disorder. I have a very low platelet count. The normal high count is between 150,000 and 450,000. My count is 7,000 to 75,000 which causes me to bleed and bruise easily. When my platelet count falls to between 10,000 and 12,000 I get a platelet transfusion to temporarily prevent bleeding.

Doctors believe I possibly got this condition from being exposed to benzene while fighting structure fires in my 30 years as a firefighter. Benzene is in many materials involved in all type of fires such as plastics, carpeting, diesel fuel, household cleaners, and so on. The disease is controlled by chemotherapy along with platelet and blood transfusions. The only thing I can say for sure about my condition is that I feel good most of the time, but when my red blood cells are low, I feel a little tired, and walking up hill or up stairs is a little more tiring, because red blood cells carry oxygen.

The only blessing about MDS is it gave me time to write these stories. When you receive 65 or 70 transfusions of chemotherapy for three hours per treatment, you can do a lot of writing, and the time flies by quickly. I am lucky so far that I have never gotten sick to my stomach or never lost my hair because of these treatments. My condition now has advanced to acute myeloid leukemia.

I have no idea what God has in store for me, but he has given me a wonderful life so far. I came from loving parents, Edwin and Catherine Slater, and I have a fantastic brother, Richard. I married my childhood sweetheart, Shirley Green, 53 years ago at the time of this writing. We have the best kids a mom and dad could ask for, Sierra Suzanne and Marc. We also have two grandchildren, Alexander, 7, and Lila, 3, in the year 2014, given to us by God and by Sierra and Phil.

We lived in beautiful Malibu, California, for some 35 years. I had a job that I loved for 30 years, and I worked with great firemen who were my brothers. I also enjoyed my hobby of racing go karts, midgets, and modifieds for some 25 years. I have had many good friends in life, including close high school classmates. I have had many experiences, some told in this book.

God may be ready to call this old fire horse home, and if that is the case, so be it. It's been a great run.

END

Lyle Slater stands in front of a Beverly Hills fire engine near the end of his career.

CPSIA information can be obtained at www.ICGtesting.com
Printed in the USA
BVOW03s2305121214

379271BV00009B/46/P